The Questions Dictionary of
HISTORY

Joy A Palmer

THE QUESTIONS PUBLISHING COMPANY LTD

BIRMINGHAM

2001

The Questions Publishing Company Ltd
27 Frederick St, Birmingham B1 3HH

First published in 2001

ISBN: 1-84190-034-6

Illustrations by Martin Cater
Cover design by Al Stewart/Martin Cater

Printed in the UK

To the teacher

This dictionary is intended to help young people understand the meaning of many of the words they will come across when studying history and the legacy of our past. It includes words relating to people and events of times gone by; also words which relate to our understanding of past civilisations and historic thinking and ideas.

The content has been chosen to include words within the capabilities of pupils in the primary and early secondary years of schooling. All words are relevant to the teaching and learning of history in the National Curriculum, notably at Key Stage 2 level.

The dictionary will make a valuable addition to any primary classroom's collection of basic reference books and to every school's library of history books. It may be made available for teaching purposes as a book, or as individual word entries, photocopied and fixed to A5 size cards. The book as a whole and its individual entries may be used in a wide variety of ways: by pupils independently or in groups, or together with the teacher. Obviously, individual words or groups of words may be the focus of a particular lesson or line of enquiry, and the dictionary as a whole can be a rich source for browsing through during spare moments.

We emphasise that this book is not simply a list of words and their definitions. Many entries go beyond the straightforward word meaning to provide some explanation, context or example as appropriate – often through the relevant illustrations. Many of the words are linked or related to others and are cross-referenced where appropriate at the heard of the entries. Where a word appears in an entry in bold type, this means that it is defined elsewhere in the dictionary. So, if pupils come across a word when studying history that they are not sure about, or introduced to in a lesson, they can look up what it means and be directed to other relevant words. They can also just pick out any word and be set on a trail of learning of facts and ideas relating to people, civilisations and major events of the past.

It is hoped that this book will lead not only to pupils' better understanding of past societies, people and events, but also to increased knowledge relating to how we know about our past and the relevance of history to our lives today.

Joy A Palmer

Dictionary Entries

Abdicate

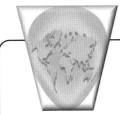

To abdicate means to give up the throne and cease to be **monarch**. Edward VIII is an example of a British monarch who chose to abdicate. Edward VIII, son of King George V, became king on his father's death in 1936. In 1937 he chose to abdicate so that he could marry a divorced American woman, Mrs Wallis Simpson.

Act of Supremacy

(see also **King Henry VIII** and **Reformation**)

King Henry VIII decided that it was in his interests to take control of the Church of England. In 1534 **parliament** passed the Act of Supremacy, which declared the king the supreme head of the Church of England. People had to take an oath accepting Henry's heirs and his supremacy in the church. The significance of this event is that it marked the break of the English Church with the Church of Rome, the Roman Catholic Church. Henry VIII denied the authority of the Pope as leader of the church.

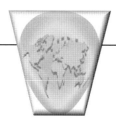

AD

(see also **BC** and **Venerable Bede**)

The letters AD stand for the Latin words Anno Domini, meaning 'in the year of our Lord'. The abbreviation AD is used to refer to dates (years) since the birth of Jesus. There is no year 0, so the year after 1BC is the year AD1. This system of dating years, called the Christian chronological system, was first adopted in the 8th century by the Venerable Bede. Generally, years before the Birth of Christ are written as the year or century BC. For years after the Birth of Christ, the year or century is written without using the letters AD. In other words, it can be taken that 'the 8th century' or '1512' are AD.

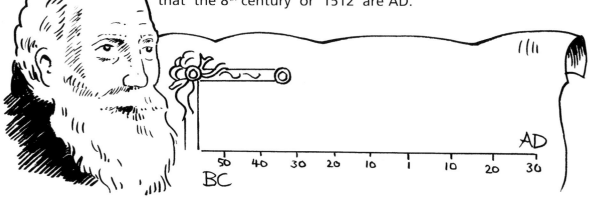

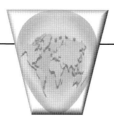

Agricultural revolution

The term agricultural revolution refers to the great changes that took place in British agriculture between the mid 18th and the mid 19th centuries. It was a time of rapidly expanding population and increased demand for food. New farming methods were introduced, resulting in enhanced crop production and improved breeds of livestock. Important developments included the invention of new ploughs and seed drills and the farming of blocks of land instead of thin strips in different fields. Further major advances took place in agriculture as a result of mechanisation in the late 19th century. The first petrol driven tractor was developed in the United States of America at the end of the 19th century.

Alexander the Great

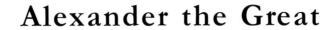

Alexander the Great, born in AD356 the son of Philip of Macedonia, became king of Macedonia at the age of twenty when his father was murdered. He was a man of tremendous courage and military skill. By the time he died of a fever at the age of thirty two, Alexander had conquered half of the known world.

Alfred the Great

(see also **Anglo-Saxons**)

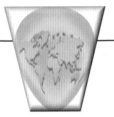

Alfred, one of the best known figures of Saxon times, was born in AD849 at Wantage. He was the youngest son of King Aethelwulf of Wessex. He ruled as king of Wessex from 871 to 899. Alfred engaged in a long battle with **Viking** invaders and eventually defeated them, saving Wessex. He adopted the title 'King of all Anglo-Saxons'. He is the only king of England to have been labelled 'the Great'. Apart from his success against invaders, Alfred is also well known for burning some cakes that he left in the oven too long.

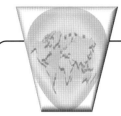

Allied Powers

(see also **First World War** and **Second World War**)

The Allied Powers is the term used to describe the twenty three countries who were united (allied) against the Central Powers of Germany, Austria-Hungary, Turkey and Bulgaria in the First World War, and the forty nine countries united against the Axis Powers of Germany, Italy and Japan in the Second World War. The twenty three Allied Powers of the First World War included France, Italy, Russia, the UK, other nations of the **Commonwealth** and, for later parts of the war, the USA. The forty nine Allied Powers of the Second World War included France, the UK, Australia and other Commonwealth nations, the USA and the USSR.

CHURCHILL   ROOSEVELT   STALIN

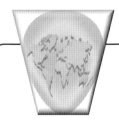

American civil war

The American civil war, or the War Between the States, took place from 1861 to1865. It was a **war** between the southern or confederate states of America, and the northern or union states. The southern states wished to keep certain rights, for example, the right to determine state law on **slavery**. They also wished to have the right to secede (withdraw) from the union. The northern states fought to maintain the union. It was a bitter and ferocious war. The first major battle was the Battle of Bull Run, which took place in Virginia in July 1861. There, the confederate army, under generals P G T Bureaugard and Thomas 'Stonewall' Jackson, forced the union army to retreat to Washington DC. Other major conflicts include the Battle of Shiloh (April 1862), the Battle of Antietam (September 1862), the Battle of Fredericksburg (December 1862), the Battle of Gettysburg (July 1863), and the Battle of Cold Harbour (June 1864). Over 600,000 soldiers were killed during the war. The union states claimed victory when the confederate troops surrendered in May 1865.

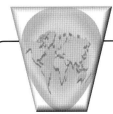

American war of independence

The American war of independence, otherwise known as the American **revolution**, took place between 1775 and 1783. It took the form of a revolt or uprising of the thirteen British north American colonies that were opposed to various aspects of British rule over them. The colonists' revolution brought about independence and resulted in the establishment of the United States of America. George Washington was elected as the first president of the USA.

GEORGE WASHINGTON

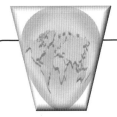

Ancient Egypt

(see also **Tutankhamun, pharaohs** and **hieroglyphics**)

The civilisation of Ancient Egypt began 7,000 years ago on the banks of the great River Nile. Early farming communities developed into tribes and established villages. In 3118BC, tribes united under the first Egyptian king, Menes. Ancient Egypt progressed from the 'old' Egyptian civilisation into the New Age, or New Kingdom of Egypt as it is often referred to by historians. The so-called New Age began around 1560BC and was the time when warrior pharaohs went into battle to win an **empire**. It was an age of war and religious conflicts, which saw the building of huge wealth as seen in temples, pyramids and treasures.

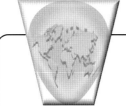

Ancient Greece

The first Greek civilisation was known as the Mycenaean, which lasted from around 1600 to 1200BC. From the 14th century BC, further invasions took place, for example, by the Dorian people in 1100BC, who founded the town of Sparta.

Between the years 750 to 550BC, the Greeks became great traders and founded many **colonies** around the coasts of the Mediterranean and the Black Sea.

Key cities in the world of Ancient Greece include Athens, Sparta, Pylos, Argos, Thebes and Corinth. Such towns were isolated, divided by mountains, with only rugged pathways between them. Towns, surrounded by farmland and barren countryside, formed what is known as 'city states'. Often, the cities had a temple dedicated to the patron god of the city, built on high ground, called an acropolis.

The modern world has gained a great **legacy** from Ancient Greek civilisation. It has had a major influence on such things as the thinking of philosophers, architecture, language, sport, science and politics.

Anglo-Saxons

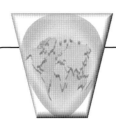

Anglo-Saxons is a general term used to describe Angles, Saxons and Jutes; Germanic invaders who conquered much of Britain between the 5th and 7th centuries. They were fierce warriors and won most battles easily. The Angles, Saxon and Jutes divided England into seven kingdoms: Northumbria, Mercia, East Anglia, Essex, Kent, Sussex and Wessex, with a ruler in charge of each.

Archaeology

(see also **evidence**)

Archaeology means the study and description of antiquities, that is, the people, relics, customs, records and monuments of ancient times. Discoveries of past remains and the scientific study of ancient monuments by archaeologists provide vital evidence of **prehistoric** society.

Archaeologists conduct 'digs' in the ground in order to unearth evidence. Every fragment found on a dig is numbered and recorded. Various items, such as pots and pieces of furniture, can be reconstructed by putting together the separate pieces that once made the whole object. Archaeologists also use a variety of scientific techniques. One of these is carbon dating. By measuring how much radioactive carbon is left in the remains of a previously living substance, such as wood from a tree, it is possible to work out when the tree died.

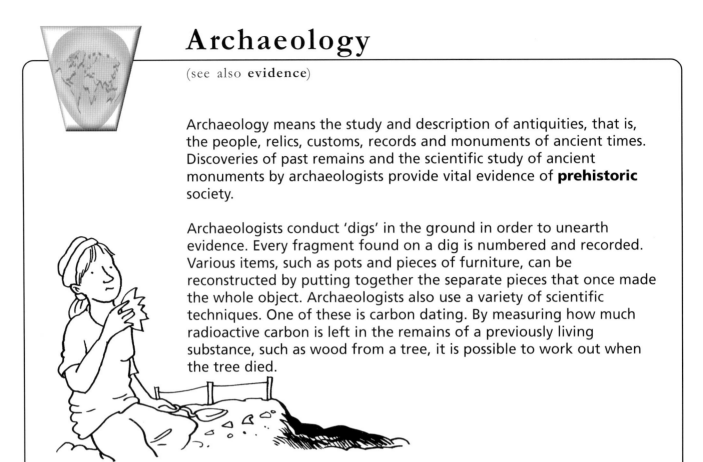

Archive

(see also **evidence**)

The term archive refers to a historical record or document that has been preserved. Archives are crucial evidence of happenings of the past. The word archive is also used to describe the place in which public records or historic documents are kept. Examples of archives include well-known documents of the past such as the **Domesday Book**, through to present day items, such as computer records and videos of events.

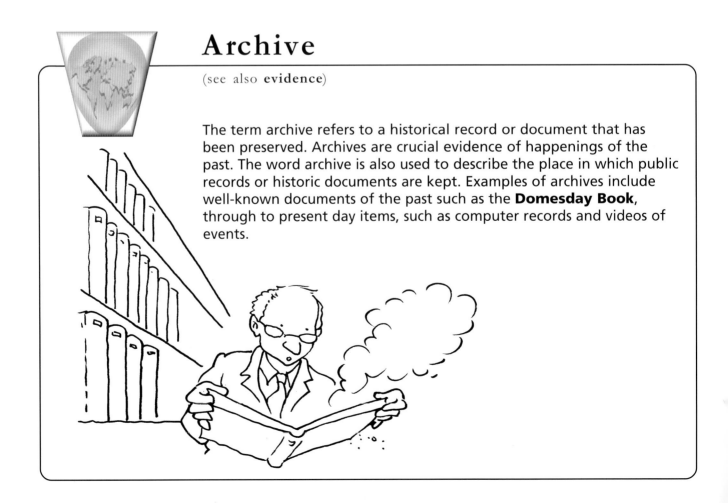

Armada

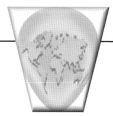

The Armada is the fleet of ships sent by the Spanish **monarch**, Philip II, to fight against England in 1588. This followed the execution of **Mary, Queen of Scots** by **Queen Elizabeth I**, a deed that angered the Roman Catholic monarchs of Europe. Furthermore, Philip II was angered by the way that Sir Francis **Drake** and other English seafarers were attacking his **colonies** and capturing his ships. The fleet consisted of 130 ships and was commanded by the Duke of Medina Sidonia. The two fleets met in the English Channel. The Spanish were defeated and less than eighty of the original Armada ships struggled back to port.

Armistice

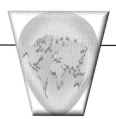

An armistice is an agreement or pact made by countries who are at war with each other to cease fighting and discuss possibilities for peace. The Armistice day at the end of the **First World War** was 11 November 1918. On this day of the year, many people today wear a red poppy as a reminder of the many men who died in combat during the world wars.

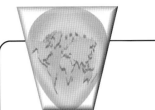

Armour

Armour is the name given to body protection worn by people fighting in battle. People of **Ancient Greece** and Rome wore armour. During the **Middle Ages**, armour called chain mail, made from interlocked chains or rings, was worn and, by the 14th century, knights went into battle completely encased in plate (metal) armour. This was extremely heavy and so not very practical. Today soldiers are protected with much lighter bullet-proof clothing.

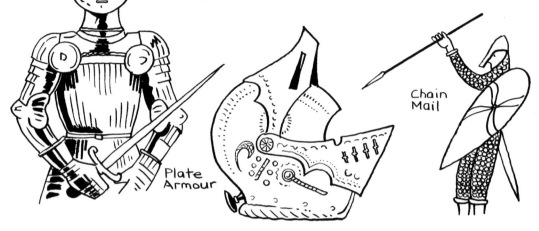

Plate Armour

Chain Mail

Artefact

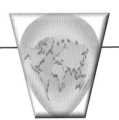

(see also **Archaeology** and **Evidence**)

An artefact (or artifact) is an artificial or man-made product. Artefacts are crucial sources of evidence of past societies. It is possible to date ancient settlements by the artefacts found on their sites. For example, artefacts dating from the time of the **Romans** would be different from those of the **Bronze Age**. The discoveries of archaeologists, such as pieces of pottery, glass, coins and jewellery, are vital artefacts that help inform us about past times.

Bronze Age Weapons

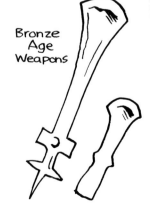

Roman Coins

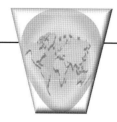

Assyrian Empire

(see also **Iron Age** and **Sumerians**)

The Assyrian Empire is one of Western Asia's great Iron Age empires. It lasted from around 2500 to 612BC in Northern Mesopotamia, now the country called Iraq. The Assyrians adopted the Sumerian structure of society and the religion that had been practised by the Sumerians. The chief god of the Assyrians was named Ashur. The empire's capital city, Ashur, was named after him. By 670BC the empire was too large to be ruled effectively. Areas such as Egypt and Babylon broke away from it. In 609BC the empire collapsed completely.

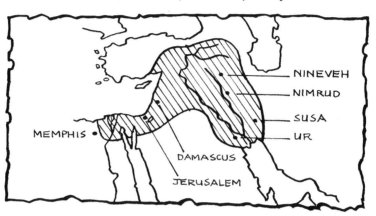

MEMPHIS

NINEVEH
NIMRUD
SUSA
UR
DAMASCUS
JERUSALEM

Aztec civilisation

(see also **Spanish Conquest**)

The Aztecs were originally wandering, hunting and farming people who arrived on the shores of Lake Taxoco in the Valley of Mexico in about AD1300. Two hundred years later, they ruled a vast empire stretching from the Pacific coast to the Gulf of Mexico. This area was inhabited by fifteen million people. The Aztec Empire possessed great power for about 100 years, until most of the civilisation was destroyed by the Spanish in the early 1500s. The Aztecs are noted for the architecture, jewellery, sculpture and textiles, the styles of which have continued to be of influence until the present day.

AZTEC
ARMY COMMANDER

AZTEC
TEXTILES

AZTEC TEMPLE

Battle of Britain

(see also **Second World War**)

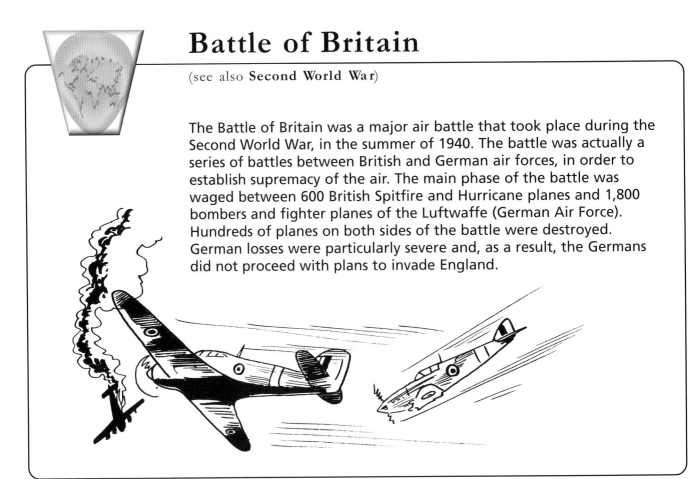

The Battle of Britain was a major air battle that took place during the Second World War, in the summer of 1940. The battle was actually a series of battles between British and German air forces, in order to establish supremacy of the air. The main phase of the battle was waged between 600 British Spitfire and Hurricane planes and 1,800 bombers and fighter planes of the Luftwaffe (German Air Force). Hundreds of planes on both sides of the battle were destroyed. German losses were particularly severe and, as a result, the Germans did not proceed with plans to invade England.

Battle of Hastings

(see also **Norman Conquest** and **Bayeux Tapestry**)

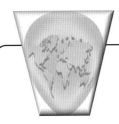

The Battle of Hastings took place on 14 October 1066. It was the famous battle in which William, Duke of Normandy, defeated King Harold and became King of England. The site of the battle is at Senlac in Sussex, six miles inland from Hastings. William's army dominated the battle and overpowered King Harold's 9,000 soldiers. This battle was a key event in British history. Kings and queens who came after William have been related to him in some way, and the event led to British society being influenced by the French culture and language.

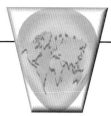

Bayeux Tapestry

(see also **Norman Conquest** and **Battle of Hastings**)

The Bayeux Tapestry is a large tapestry (woven fabric), which records in pictures the NORMAN invasion of England in 1066. Work on the tapestry began in 1080. It represents a very important source of historic **evidence** that helps us understand events of the Norman invasion and conquest. Today the tapestry may be seen in the Bayeux Museum.

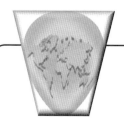

BC

(see also **AD**)

The letters BC stand for 'before Christ'. They are used to denote years or centuries in the Christian chronological system of numbering years that were before the Birth of Christ.

Benin

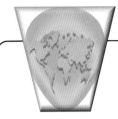

Benin is the name of a former important African Kingdom. The Kingdom of Benin lasted from 1200 until 1897. It was at the height of its power between 1400 and the mid 17th century, when it ruled the area between the Niger Delta and Lagos. The kingdom traded in ivory, palm oil, spices and slaves. When the kingdom declined, it became a province of Nigeria. The ruler of Benin today, known as the oba, rules as a supreme or divine **monarch**.

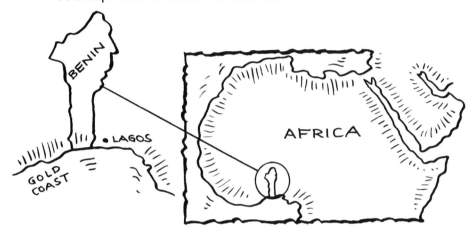

Black Death

(see also **Great Plague**)

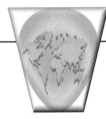

In 1348 a great epidemic of a deadly disease known as the Black Death, or bubonic plague, began to sweep across Europe. In Britain, around a third of the population died from the Black Death in eighteen months. The cause of the plague was a bacterium that was transmitted by fleas that were carried into Europe by migrating black rats from Asia.

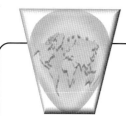

Blitz

(see also **Battle of Britain**)

When the Battle of Britain was over, German bombers began night-time raids on Britain. This period was known as the Blitz. It continued until the spring of 1941. In retaliation, Britain and the USA bombed Germany and targets in German occupied territories. A second blitz took place between 1944 and 1945, when the south of England was bombed by Germany.

Many civilians died or were injured during the blitz when areas of large British cities, such as London and Coventry, were destroyed. During the raids, people took refuge in air raid shelters where they were less likely to be killed than in rooms of their houses.

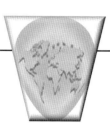

British Empire

(see also **Empire, Colonies** and **Commonwealth**)

The British Empire is the term used to describe all of the various territories around the world that were won in **conquest** or colonised by Britain from around 1600 onwards. The British Empire was at its largest around 1920, when it included over a quarter of the area and population of the world. The Commonwealth comprises some of the former and remaining Empire territories. Most original British Empire territories are now either independent states, or are ruled by other powers.

■ BRITISH EMPIRE
CIRCA 1886

Bronze Age

The Bronze Age describes the period of time from about 2100BC when people used bronze. This is a metal, made by mixing copper with tin. Bronze was an important discovery as it enabled metalsmiths to make much stronger tools, weapons and other implements, including those used in agriculture. During the Bronze Age, people lived in small villages in huts made out of interwoven twigs covered with mud. Many of the small settlements belonged to a larger community, ruled by a chief.

Buddhism

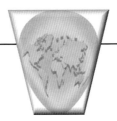

Buddhism is the name of a religion that originated in India about 500BC. Buddhism derives from the teachings of the Buddha. Buddhists do not worship gods. The central belief is Karma or destiny. Good or evil deeds performed by people are rewarded or punished either in this life or in a future life.

RECLINING BUDDAH, THAILAND

BUDDHIST MONK

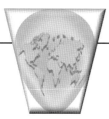

Byzantine Empire

The Byzantine Empire, or the Eastern Roman Empire, lasted from 395 to 1453. Its capital was at Constantinople, formerly called Byzantium, and today Istanbul. The Byzantine Empire reached the height of its influence and prosperity under the Macedonian **dynasty**, from 867 to 1056. The **legacy** of the empire includes many works of art and architecture found throughout Europe.

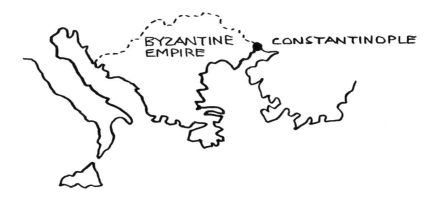

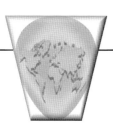

Caesar, Julius

(see also **Romans** and **Roman conquest**)

Gaius Julius Caesar was a Roman statesman and general, who lived from 100BC to 44BC. In 55BC he led the invasion into Britain, which marked the beginning of the Roman conquest.

On 15 March 44BC, Caesar was stabbed to death by conspirators at the foot of the statue of his former rival Pompey, in Rome.

Caesar's adopted son Augustus assumed the name of Caesar and passed it on to his adopted son Tiberius. From then on it was used by successive emperors and it became the title of the Roman rulers.

Captain Cook

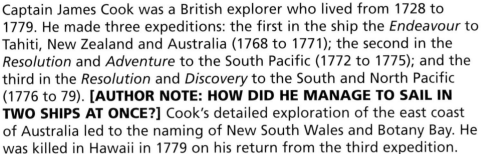

Captain James Cook was a British explorer who lived from 1728 to 1779. He made three expeditions: the first in the ship the *Endeavour* to Tahiti, New Zealand and Australia (1768 to 1771); the second in the *Resolution* and *Adventure* to the South Pacific (1772 to 1775); and the third in the *Resolution* and *Discovery* to the South and North Pacific (1776 to 79). **[AUTHOR NOTE: HOW DID HE MANAGE TO SAIL IN TWO SHIPS AT ONCE?]** Cook's detailed exploration of the east coast of Australia led to the naming of New South Wales and Botany Bay. He was killed in Hawaii in 1779 on his return from the third expedition.

Castles

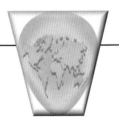

A castle is a large fortified building or set of buildings. Most castles were built as the private fortress of a **sovereign** or member of the **nobility**. In Britain, the earliest castles were built during the time of the **Norman conquest**. They consisted of an earth mound with wooden buildings surrounded by a wall and a ditch. Later castles were built of stone. Castle building in Britain was at its peak in the 13th century. Remains of many castles can be visited today, particularly in Wales and Northumbria. They provide important **evidence** of **medieval** society.

STONE CASTLE

MOTTE & BAILEY

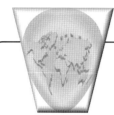

Celts

(see also **Iron Age**)

Celts were the first people to inhabit central Europe after 1000BC. The Celts first came to Britain in about 500BC. It is thought that the technique of smelting iron may have been introduced in Britain by the Celtic people. The **legacy** of the Celtic people continues to this day in the form of legends and influence on art and music.

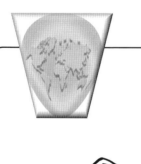

Charlemagne

(see also **Holy Roman Empire**)

King Charlemagne, or Charles I the Great, lived from AD742 to 814. In AD768 he became king of the Franks. He was successful in the **conquest** of a great deal of Europe and he became its first great leader since the fall of the **Roman Empire**. In AD800, Charlemagne was crowned Holy Roman Emperor by Pope Leo III.

Christianity

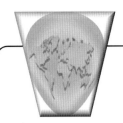

Christianity is a religion that originated in Palestine. It is based on the teachings of a person named Jesus of Nazareth, who is called Christ, the Son of God, by his followers. Christendom is a word used to refer to the Christian domain, or followers of Christ collectively.

Chronology

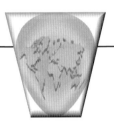

Chronology is the science of computing time or periods of time, and of attributing events to their true dates. A chronological table of historic events sets out events in correct sequence or chronological order.

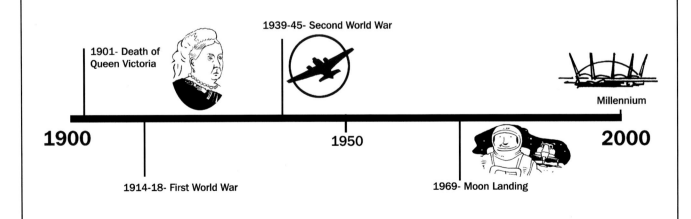

1901- Death of Queen Victoria

1939-45- Second World War

Millennium

1900   1950   2000

1914-18- First World War

1969- Moon Landing

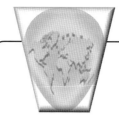

Churchill, Winston

(see also **Second World War**)

Winston Churchill was a famous British Conservative politician **[AUTHOR NOTE: BUT DIDN'T HE 'CROSS THE FLOOR' ONCE OR TWICE DURING HIS TIME?]** who lived from 1874 to 1965. He was prime minister from 1940 to 1945, a time of crucial importance as this was the period of the Second World War. He returned to office as prime minister from 1951 to 1955. Churchill is regarded as a great statesman and able politician. He negotiated with other leaders of the **Allied Powers** the unconditional surrender of Germany at the end of the Second World War.

Civil rights

Civil rights are the rights of an individual citizen. Some countries are very specific about civil rights and write them into legislation. For example, the Bill of Rights in the constitution of the United States of America guarantees by law that all citizens will have equal treatment. Civil rights have been fought for throughout history. One famous rights campaigner was the black leader and Baptist minister Martin Luther King who lived in the USA from 1929 to 1968.

MARTIN LUTHER KING

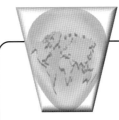

Colonies

(see also **Empire**)

A colony is a territory separated from the country that rules it. Colonies were set up all over the world by Britain as the **British Empire** was expanded. Former British colonies, now independent countries, include India, Pakistan, Sri Lanka, Cyprus, Tanzania, Jamaica, Uganda, Kenya, Malaysia, Malawi, Malta, Zambia, Singapore, Bangladesh and Zimbabwe. The word colony is also used to refer to a group of people know as 'colonists' who settle in a territory far away from their homeland. The colonists form a community, connected politically to their home country.

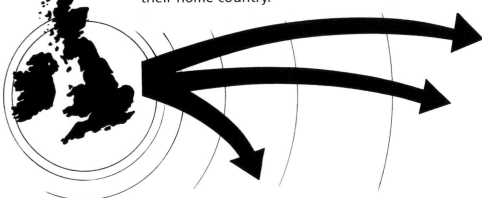

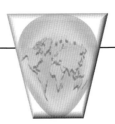

Columbus, Christopher

Christopher Columbus was born in Italy in 1451. He is the famous explorer and navigator who discovered the American continent. Columbus made four key voyages to the so called New World: in 1492 to 1493 to San Salvador Island, Cuba and Haiti; 1493 to 1496 to Guadeloupe, Montserrat, Antigua, Puerto Rico and Jamaica; 1498 to the South American mainland and Trinidad; and 1502 to 1504 to Honduras and Nicaragua. Christopher Columbus' flagship was the *Santa Maria*. Her two accompanying ships were the *Pinta* and the *Nina*.

1ST VOYAGE ___

- - - -
3RD VOYAGE

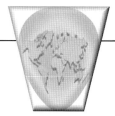

Commonwealth

(see also **British Empire**)

The British Commonwealth is an association of fifty countries and their dependencies (states controlled by them), who were once a part of the British Empire and are now independent. The Commonwealth also includes some territories that remain as dependencies of Britain. Membership of the Commonwealth is voluntary. Its heads of government meet regularly. It has no formal constitution.

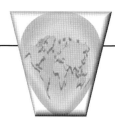

Communism

Communism is a political ideology or set of ideas based on the theories of a man named Karl Marx. Marx, a German philosopher and economist, lived from 1818 to 1883. He believed that a society should be based on the principle of common ownership. The world's first communist state was the **Russian Empire**, which later became the Soviet Union. All of the countries in eastern Europe became communist after the **Second World War** as a result of Russian influence.

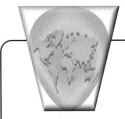

Conflict

A conflict is a fight or lengthy struggle, often (in historical circumstances) involving weapons and arms. An example of a present day conflict is that taking place in Kosovo, a region in South Serbia. **[AUTHOR NOTE: IF THIS CONFLICT ENDS, THE BOOK WILL BE DATED]**

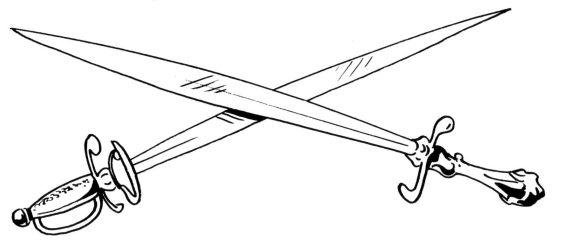

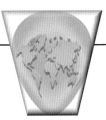

Conquest

(see also **Norman Conquest**, **Roman Conquest** and **Spanish Conquest**)

A conquest is the act of gaining control of a territory or society by armed force. It means overcoming, or gaining victory over an enemy.

Court

(see also **Sovereign**)

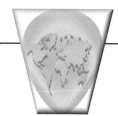

A Court is a name given to a place where a sovereign lives and 'holds state', that is, exercises rule and government attended by such people as ministers and councillors. Throughout history, people have lived and worked in the society of a Court, including the advisers to the sovereign or courtiers.

Crimean War

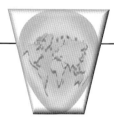

The Crimean War took place between 1853 and 1856. It was a war between the **Allied Powers** of England, France, Turkey and Sardinia, against Russia. Famous battles of the war include battles of the River Alma, Balaclava and Inkerman. The war ended with the defeat of Russia and with the signing of the Treaty of Paris in 1856. One positive outcome of this war was a great improvement in medical services for the British Army. The campaign to improve military nursing services was led by Florence Nightingale, a famous pioneer in the field of medicine.

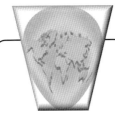

Cromwell, Oliver

(see also **English civil war** and **King Charles I**)

Oliver Cromwell lived from 1599 to 1658. He was the leader of the parliamentary side of the struggles against King Charles I in the English civil war. He led the parliamentarians to victory in the Battle of Marston Moor in 1644 and the Battle of Naseby in 1645. At Naseby, the parliamentarians won control of the country. Following the death of the king in 1649, Cromwell set up and became head of a **republic** known as the Commonwealth in England. From 1653 he made himself ruler, with the title Lord Protector.

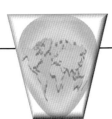

Crusades

Between the 11th and the 15th centuries, a series of military expeditions called crusades was undertaken by Christian European powers. The original aim of the crusades, or holy wars, was to recapture Palestine (the Holy Land) from Muslim Turks. New orders of soldier-monks were established to engage in fighting. These included the Knights of St John, founded in 1098.

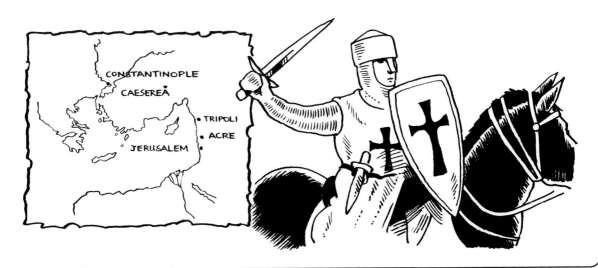

da Vinci, Leonardo

(see also **Renaissance**)

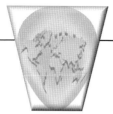

Leonardo da Vinci was one of the greatest men of the Renaissance period. He was an Italian artist and inventor who lived from 1452 to 1519. He studied nature and the form of the human body in order to draw living forms more accurately. One of his most famous paintings is called the *Mona Lisa*.

Democracy

Democracy means government by the people, or by their elected representatives. Within a democracy, it is recognised and accepted that all people should have equal rights and privileges. In some nations of the present day world, people are still campaigning and fighting for such democratic rights.

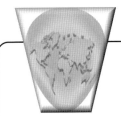

Dictatorship

A dictatorship is a political situation in which a state or country is ruled by a dictator. A dictator is a supreme authority who has the absolute power to rule or deal with a crisis. Many dictatorships arose at the end of the **First World War**. Examples of dictators include **Mussolini**, Franco, **Hitler** and **Stalin**.

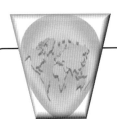

Dissolution of the monasteries

(see also **King Henry VIII** and **Monastery**)

Between the years 1536 and 1539, King Henry VIII closed down all the convents and monasteries in England. Many of them were sold and numerous others destroyed. This is known as the period of the dissolution of the monasteries. The king's excuse for doing this was that the monasteries, according to him, were corrupt or not viable because of lack of money.

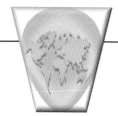

Domesday Book

The Domesday Book is a record of a survey, called the Domesday Survey, carried out in England in 1086. The survey recorded the details of all land holdings in the country. It was ordered by the king, William I, so that he could make an assessment of the wealth of each area of the country, and then decide what taxes should be paid. The Domesday Book is still in existence and is a very important historical record, showing that many of our present day **settlements** existed a century ago.

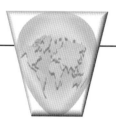

Drake, Francis

(see also **Queen Elizabeth I** and **Armada**)

Francis Drake, who lived from 1545 until 1596, was a famous English explorer. He was the second person in the world to sail right the way around it. (The first circumnavigation was by the Portuguese explorer, **Ferdinand Magellan**.) Drake's famous voyage was requested by Queen Elizabeth I and was undertaken between the years 1577 to 1580 in a ship called *The Golden Hind*. Francis Drake was also involved in helping to defeat the Spanish in the Armada in 1588. He was knighted by the queen as a recognition of his endeavours at sea, therefore becoming Sir Francis Drake.

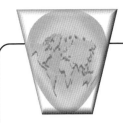

Dynasty

(see also **Houses of History**)

A dynasty is a succession of rulers of the same line or family. For example, the dynasty of the **Tudors** in British history included Henry VII, Henry VIII, Edward VI, Mary I and Elizabeth I.

HENRY VII

EDWARD VI

HENRY VIII

MARY I

ELIZABETH I

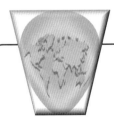

Emperor Augustus

Augustus, who lived from 63BC to AD14, was the first of the **Roman** emperors. He bore the title of Octavian and was emperor from 27BC. Octavian married a niece of **Julius Caesar** and became Caesar's adopted son and heir. In 27BC he was given the title of Augustus, meaning 'venerable'.

The rule of Emperor Augustus brought an end to the Roman **republic** with elected leaders. A peaceful **empire** was established in its place.

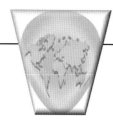

Empire

(see also **Assyrian Empire**, **British Empire**, **Byzantine Empire**, **Holy Roman Empire**, **Mogul Empire** and **Ottoman Empire**)

An empire is an extensive territory, perhaps an aggregate of many states, ruled over by an emperor or by a **sovereign** state. The emperor has supreme control over the empire.

ROMAN EMPIRE AROUND 120 AD

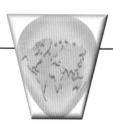

English civil war

(see also **King Charles I** and Oliver **Cromwell**)

The English civil war lasted from 1625 until 1649. As a whole, it was a long series of tensions, struggles and battles. The first key event of the war was the Battle of Edgehill, which took place in 1641. The war was a long conflict between King Charles I and the royalists or cavaliers on one side, and the parliamentarians or roundheads, headed up by Oliver Cromwell, on the other. It was a major struggle over the powers of the king and the powers of **parliament**. Eventually, the royalists were defeated. King Charles I was executed in 1649.

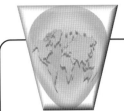

English Renaissance

(see also **Renaissance**)

The term English Renaissance refers to the period during the reign of **Queen Elizabeth I** when the arts flourished. Influential names associated with the English Renaissance include William Shakespeare (1564 to 1616) and Christopher Marlowe (1564 to 1593), both famous writers, the composer William Byrd (1543 to 1623), and the artist Nicholas Hilliard (1547 to 1619).

WILLIAM SHAKESPEARE

THE GLOBE THEATRE

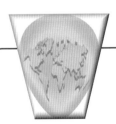

European Union

The European Union is an association of countries in the continent of Europe. The six original members – Belgium, France, West Germany, Italy, Luxembourg and the Netherlands – were joined by the UK, Denmark and the Republic of Ireland in 1973, Greece in 1981, Spain and Portugal in 1986, East Germany in 1990 (on reunification of Germany), and Austria, Finland and Sweden in 1995. Other countries await full membership. Aims of the European Union include the expansion of trade, the encouragement of free movement of capital and human resources within the association and the creation of a closer union or community among the people of Europe.

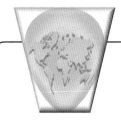

Evidence

(see also **History**, **Artefact**, **Archaeology** and **Archive**)

The phrases 'evidence of the past' and 'historic evidence' refer to the wide range of sources of proof that past events took place in human society. Archives are vital sources of evidence. Various examples of historic evidence are referred to in other entries in this book, for example the pictorial evidence in the **Bayeux Tapestry**, the archaeological finds of the **Indus Valley**, the writings of the **Venerable Bede**, and the objects and artefacts found in the tomb of **Tutankhamun**.

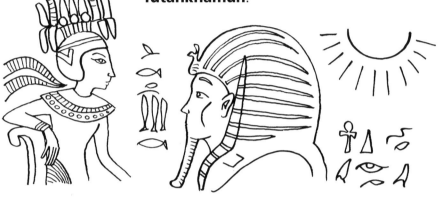

Factory

(see also **Factory Act**)

A factory is a building or buildings with the necessary machinery or equipment for the manufacture of goods.

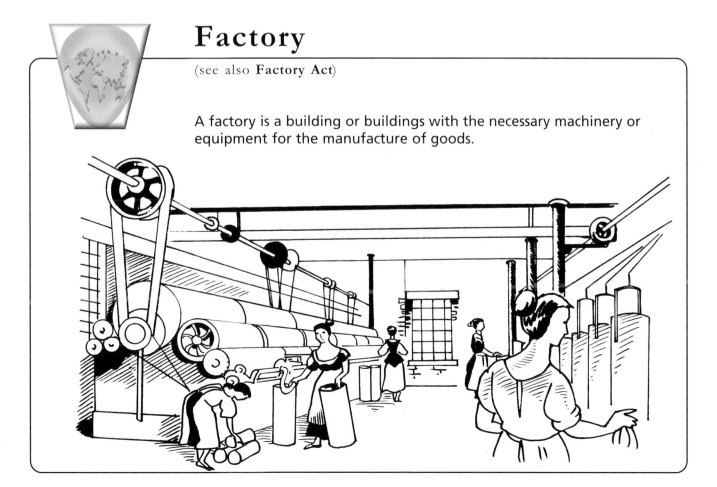

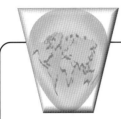

Factory Act

(see also **Factory**)

A Factory Act is an act of parliament that governs conditions of work, hours of labour, and aspects of health and safety of employees at work.

From the start of the 19th century in Britain, people campaigned to improve the long working hours, unhealthy conditions and very poor pay endured by those who worked in factories and mines. Campaigns were also waged to ban the employment of young children.

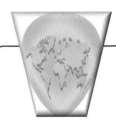

The first act of its kind to be passed was the Health and Morals of Apprentices Act of 1802. In 1833 the first factory inspectors were appointed. By the end of the 19th century, a lower age limit of 11 had been set for the employment of children.

Farming

(see also **Agricultural Revolution**)

Farming is the business of cultivating land and raising livestock in order to provide food. The first farmers arrived in Britain around 4000BC. They cleared land to graze animals and grow food. Farming methods have changed very considerably through the centuries and particularly from the time of the Agricultural Revolution.

Fascism

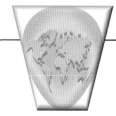

(see also **Mussolini**)

Fascism was originally the name of the political movement in power in Italy from 1925 to 1943 under the leadership of Mussolini. The name fascism comes from the Latin word 'fasces', which referred to the wooden torches that became the symbol of the fascist political party.

Fascism supported **nationalism** and **imperialism**, and was strongly opposed to **communism** and **democracy**. Later the name was also applied to other nationalistic movements, such as German National Socialism (party of the **nazis**).

Fawkes, Guy

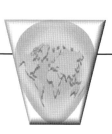

(see also **Gunpowder Plot**)

Guy Fawkes was a Catholic conspirator who played a major role in the gunpowder plot in 1605. The plot was discovered in a cellar underneath the Houses of Parliament, where Fawkes was hiding with a large store of explosives. Guy Fawkes was arrested and later executed.

His name and the plot are still remembered every year on the day of its anniversary, 5 November. The day is known as Guy Fawkes Day or Bonfire Night. People light bonfires and fireworks, and burn a 'Guy'.

Feudalism

(see also **Normans**)

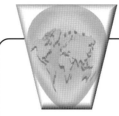

Feudalism is the name used to describe a system of organising society that was introduced in England by the Normans. The system involves a complicated series of duties, rights and loyalties. For example, everyone owed ultimate loyalty to the king; large areas of land, called fiefs, were granted by the king to his chief nobles; the nobles granted smaller areas of land, called manors, to knights; and the knights granted small areas of land to peasants. Various dues were paid for the land made available in each case.

First World War

(see also **Allied Powers**)

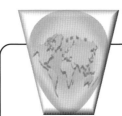

The First World War lasted from 1914 until 1918. It was a **war** between the Central European Powers of Germany, Austria, Hungary, Turkey and Bulgaria, and the Allied Powers. It took only three weeks in July and August 1914 for almost all of the major countries in Europe to become involved in this bitter and fierce war. Many civilians were called to fight in the war. A good deal of the fighting took place in ground trenches in northern France. It is estimated that ten million lives were lost as a result of the fighting, and many more millions were wounded. Fighting stopped late in 1918, and the war finally ended with the signing of a peace treaty known as the Treaty of Versailles in 1919.

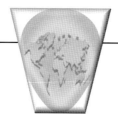

French Revolution

(see also **Napoleon I**)

The period of the French Revolution lasted from 1789 until 1799. During this time, the people of France overthrew their **monarch** and the country became a **republic**. It was a period of great violence, with riots and bitter struggles in France, and attacks by other nations. King Louis XVI was condemned to death in December 1792 and executed in January 1793. His death was followed by a further period of great violence, known as the Reign of Terror. The revolution ended when Napoleon overcame the rulers in 1799 and seized power as dictator.

ROBESPIERRE

MARAT

Government

The Government is the body of persons who are charged with the duties and responsibilities of governing. That is, they are charged with ruling over and managing the affairs and actions of people in a particular country or locality.

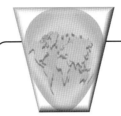

Great Exhibition

The Victorian 'Great Exhibition' opened on 1 May 1851. The idea to hold this 'Great Exhibition of the Works of Industry of All Nations' was mainly that of Prince Albert, consort of **Queen Victoria**. It was housed in and around the specially constructed Crystal Palace building. The exhibition demonstrated the importance of trade and industry of Victorian times. There were over 100,000 exhibits including railway engines, ships, agricultural implements, household machines, clocks, furniture and countless tools and gadgets.

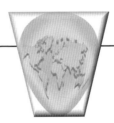

Great Fire of London

The Great Fire of London broke out in 1666, the year after the tragedy caused by the **Great Plague**. The city was destroyed by the fire, which raged uncontrolled for four days. The fire was extremely fast spreading and impossible to control because of the many wooden buildings of the city that were crowded close together in the streets.

SAMUEL PEPYS

Great Plague

(see also **Black Death**)

In 1665, an epidemic of Bubonic plague broke out in England. Like the Black Death before it, the plague was carried by rats. The Great Plague killed 68,000 people in London alone. The plague spread extremely fast as a result of crowded living conditions of the day, poor hygiene, little medical care and lack of available cure. Any house with a sick person had a cross painted on the door as a warning sign to passers by. The call of "bring out your dead" was frequently heard in the streets.

Gunpowder Plot

(see also **Guy Fawkes**)

The term the Gunpowder Plot refers to an event in British history when a group of Catholics conspired to blow up **King James I** and his parliament. It took place on 5 November 1605. The leading conspirator was Guy Fawkes. The plot was discovered because of an anonymous letter telling that the Houses of Parliament were to be blown up.

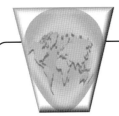

Heraldry

Heraldry is the term that refers to the symbols and insignia that represent a family, **dynasty**, individual or realm. Early examples of heraldry are the simple symbols that were put on shields and banners in order for them to be recognised in battles. In later years, heraldry became increasingly complex. During the 14th century special 'courts of chivalry' were set up to oversee and regulate it.

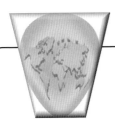

Hieroglyphics

(see also **Ancient Egypt**)

The people of Ancient Egypt introduced a form of 'writing' called hieroglyphics. Hieroglyphics are picture signs, often used to 'spell out' words. There were over 700 of these symbols. Some hieroglyphics are read from top to bottom, while others can be read from left to right or vice versa. A Frenchman, Jean-Francois Champollion, solved the code of the hieroglyphics in 1882 with the aid of the Rosetta Stone – a stone bearing the same message in two different languages, Egyptian and Greek.

Hinduism

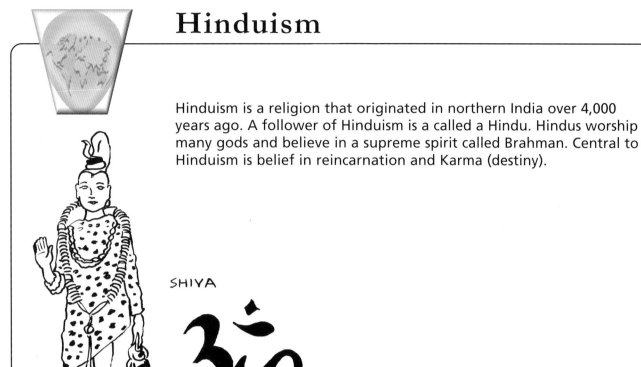

Hinduism is a religion that originated in northern India over 4,000 years ago. A follower of Hinduism is a called a Hindu. Hindus worship many gods and believe in a supreme spirit called Brahman. Central to Hinduism is belief in reincarnation and Karma (destiny).

SHIVA

Hiroshima

(see also **Second World War**)

Hiroshima is a port and industrial city on the south coast of Honshu Island, Japan. It is famous because it was destroyed by the first wartime use of an atomic bomb. On 6 August 1945, the USA dropped the bomb in order to bring about the end of the Second World War. Over four square miles of the city were totally destroyed and damage spread much further afield. 78,150 people of Hiroshima were found dead after the explosion and others died later. Many thousands of people were injured and suffered long term effects of radiation.

A second atomic bomb was dropped on the Japanese town of Nagasaki on 9 August 1945. Japan surrendered on 14 August 1945, and the war ended on 2 September 1945.

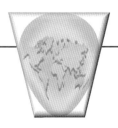

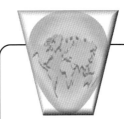

History

(see also **Evidence**)

History is the record of events that have happened in human societies. It is the study of the past and past societies. History includes events of very long ago (ancient history) and events of the very recent past – even yesterday is history. Understanding the past depends on evidence and records. It is very important that evidence is reliable if a true understanding of historic events is to be gained. Many accounts of the past depend upon individual viewpoints and interpretation, and two accounts of the same event may not necessarily agree with each other.

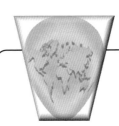

Hitler

(see also **Second World War, Nazis, Allied Powers** and **Holocaust**)

Adolf Hitler lived from 1889 to 1945. He was the Führer, or leader of the nazi party, in Germany from 1921. From 1933 Hitler was Chancellor of Germany and became Head of State, acting as a **dictator** from 1934. Hitler and **Mussolini** formed an alliance in 1936 and were joined by Japan in 1940 in their fight to win the Second World War. Hitler was therefore the leader of the forces opposing the Allied Powers. He was responsible, with other nazis, for the holocaust. Adolf Hitler committed suicide on 30 April 1945.

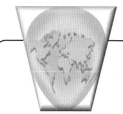

Holocaust

(see also **Nazis**, **Hitler** and **Second World War**)

The Holocaust is the term used to describe the atrocities (dreadful things) done by the nazis to millions of people. They imprisoned, tortured and exterminated (murdered) people who they believed to be unwanted or undesirable in the world. In particular, they killed millions of Jews. Many people were taken to prison camps, such as Belsen and Auschwitz, and **evidence** from these places of death and torture remains as a horrific reminder of the atrocities committed there.

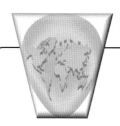

Holy Roman Empire

(see also **Christianity**, **Charlemagne** and **Empire**)

The Holy Roman Empire was the empire of King Charlemagne, who was crowned as its emperor in AD800 by Pope Leo III. Charlemagne forced all the people he conquered to become Christians. In particular he fought Muslim people of the **Islamic** religion who were invading southern Europe at the time. The expansion of the Holy Roman Empire was regarded as a Christian revival of the **Roman Empire**, which is why the term 'holy' was used to describe it.

HOLY ROMAN EMPIRE

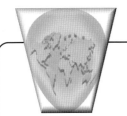

Houses of history

(see also **Dynasty**)

The houses of history in Britain are the family names of the **monarchs**. British Houses of History in **chronological** order from the time of the **Norman conquest** are: **Normans** (1066 to 1154); House of Plantagenets (1154 to 1399); House of Lancaster (1399 to 1461); House of York (1461 to 1485); House of **Tudor** (1485 to 1603); House of **Stuart** (1603 to 1714); House of Hanover (1714 to 1837); House of Saxe-Coburg-Gotha (1837 to 1910), and House of **Windsor** (1910 to the present day).

GEORGE I - HANOVER

JAMES I - STUART

EDWARD IV - YORK

HENRY VIII - TUDOR

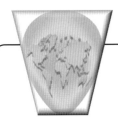

Hundred Years War

The so-called Hundred Years War was actually a series of wars that took place between England and France between 1337 and 1453. The wars began after the death of Charles IV of France who died without a male heir. In 1337, war broke out when the king of England, Edward III, whose mother was Isabelle of France, tried to claim the French throne. England won many victories during the series of wars, but by the end of the battles in 1453, England had lost all of its land in France with the exception of Calais.

Imperialism

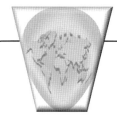

(see also **Empire** and **Colonies**)

Imperialism is the political policy of extending the power and authority of a ruler or government beyond the boundaries of a single country. The growth and development of empires, such as the **British Empire**, is an example of imperialism. Imperialistic rule may involve direct rule over other places, or control of such matters as trade and markets for goods. Another name for imperialism is colonialism, involving the establishment and rule of colonies by an empire.

EMPEROR HADRIAN

HADRIAN'S WALL

Incas

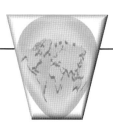

Incas were tribal people who belonged to the ancient civilisation of Peru. The civilisation began high in the Andes mountains. The first Inca ruler lived around AD1200. In 1438, a man called Pachacutec became their emperor and the Incas spread out from the city of Cuzco, their capital, to conquer a huge empire. The empire lasted about a hundred years before the Spanish conquered the Incas. The emperor of the Incas was called 'the Inca'. His people believed that he was a descendent of the Sun.

INCA EMPIRE

CUZCO

Indigenous people

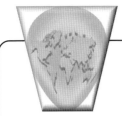

Indigenous people are those who are native to a particular region. That is, they belong naturally there. They, and their ancestors were born in the place in question, and their ancestors were the original inhabitants of their lands. Indigenous people include the South Western Indians of North America (Apache), the plains Indians of North America (Sioux), the Inuit (Eskimo) people of Canada, the Aborigines of Australia, and the Maoris of New Zealand.

Indus Valley

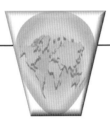

The Indus Valley lies in present day Pakistan. It gave its name to the Indus Valley civilisation, one of the four ancient civilisations of the world. The civilisation lasted from its origins, around 3000BC, until its collapse around 1700BC. Archaeological excavations have provided much **evidence** about life in the two main cities of the ancient civilisation, Mohenjo Daro and Harappa. Archaeological discoveries include planned streets with drainage, baths, temples and various other buildings and **artefacts**.

REMAINS OF MOHENJO DARO

INDUS

MOHENJO DARO

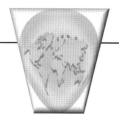

Industrial revolution

The industrial revolution was a time of very rapid development of industry in Britain through the invention and introduction of machines into factories. An example of a major invention of the time is the steam engine. Some of Britain's major cities, such as Birmingham, Manchester and Leeds, developed during the period of the industrial revolution, which took place from around 1750 and lasted throughout the 19th century. Britain was the first country to experience such rapid industrial change. From 1830 to the early 20th century the revolution spread throughout Europe and the USA, also to Japan and British **colonies**.

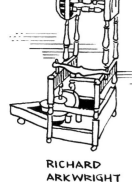

RICHARD ARKWRIGHT

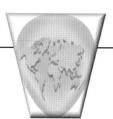

Interpretation

(see also **Evidence** and **History**)

Interpretation means the act of explaining or finding meaning. Historians interpret evidence in order to explain and describe historic events. Interpretation depends on the viewpoint or evidence available to an individual historian. Hence one person's account of a past event may not necessarily be exactly the same as another's.

Invasion

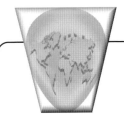

An invasion is an aggressive entrance or intrusion into a country or locality by hostile forces from elsewhere. The word is generally used to describe the act of invading enemy territory by armed forces. An example of an invasion is the German invasion of Poland in September 1939, marking the commencement of the **Second World War**.

Iron Age

(see also **Celts**)

The Iron Age is so called because it was the age when early people first used the technique of smelting iron, probably introduced by the Celts. This technique reached Britain around 700BC. During the early years of the Iron Age, people lived in villages or on farms. In later years, larger settlements known as oppida were established. The people belonged to tribes, ruled by chiefs.

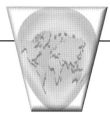

Islam

Islam is the name of the religion founded in Mecca, Arabia, by the prophet Muhammad in the early 7th century AD. Followers of the Islamic faith are called Muslims. The sacred book of Islam is the Koran. All Muslims are meant to visit Mecca at least once in their lives. Muslims should pray five times every day, facing towards Mecca.

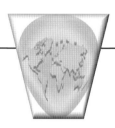

King Arthur

King Arthur is a legendary hero who is believed to have battled against the Saxon invasion. Some historians believe that King Arthur did exist. It is documented that he was born at Tintagel Castle in Cornwall, to a father who was King of the Britons. He became king at the age of fifteen on the death of his father. Many legends were written about him. It is suggested that he won countless battles, aided by Caliburn (or Excalibur), his special sword, a gift from the Lady of the Lake.

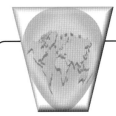

King Charles I

(see also **Stuarts**, **English civil war** and Oliver **Cromwell**)

King Charles I of England lived from 1600 to 1649 and came to the throne in 1625, the son of **King James I**. Charles was an unpopular king with his **parliament** as he believed that no-one had any right to question what he did. As a result of various disagreements, the country divided itself into two – those who supported the king (royalists) and those who supported parliament (parliamentarians). Civil war broke out, and Charles was eventually defeated by the opposition, headed up by Oliver Cromwell, in 1645. The king was brought to trial in 1648 and was condemned to death. He was executed in 1649.

SEAL OF CHARLES I

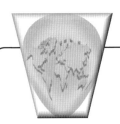

King Edward I

King Edward I lived from 1239 to 1307 and was king of England from 1272. He was son of King Henry III and a member of the Plantagenet **house of history**. Edward's ambition was to extend his rule to Wales and Scotland. He conquered Wales by 1283 and had nine huge **castles** built throughout north Wales, including those at Harlech, Conway and Caernarvon. Edward failed to gain total control of Scotland, although he engaged in many battles, some of which he won. His attempts to conquer Scotland led to his being nicknamed 'Hammer of the Scots'.

CONWY CASTLE

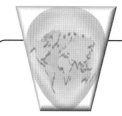

King Henry VII

(see also **Tudors**)

King Henry VII, or Henry Tudor, lived from 1457 to 1509. He was the first of the **Tudor monarchs** of England. He came to the throne in 1485. In 1486, Henry married Elizabeth of York. This marriage united the rival houses of Lancaster and York, and Henry restored peace after the **wars of the roses**.

Henry VII was a popular and hard-working king. He was also a good businessman. He avoided foreign wars and his reign is noted for bringing peace and prosperity to England.

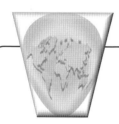

King Henry VIII

(see also **Tudors**, **Act of Supremacy** and **Dissolution of the monasteries**)

King Henry VIII of England lived from 1491 until 1547. He became king in 1509. Henry was a handsome and high-spirited king, noted for the large number of wives he had, six in total. They were (in order of marriage), Catherine of Aragon, Ann Boleyn, Jane Seymour, Anne of Cleves, Catherine Howard and Catherine Parr. Other than these various marriages, the reign of King Henry VIII is noted for its foreign wars and religious upheaval. He took control of the Church of England in the Act of Supremacy.

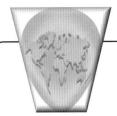

King James VI & I

(see also **Stuarts**, **Mary, Queen of Scots** and **Gunpowder Plot**)

King James I of England, Son of Mary, Queen of Scots, lived from 1566 until 1625. He became King of England in 1603. He had been King of Scotland as James VI from 1567. In 1603 the two thrones were united. James I was not a popular king. He was known to have favourites among his friends, who he promoted to powerful positions, and he regarded himself as a supreme or divine ruler (i.e. accountable only to God), whose views and decisions could not be challenged by anyone. James I was also very extravagant, and he imposed heavy taxation and duties on the country without the approval of parliament.

[Alternative: In 1603 the two thrones of England and Scotland were united when King James VI of Scotland, son of Mary Queen of Scots, was made heir to the English throne by Elizabeth I and became King James I of Great Britain and Ireland. He lived from from 1566 until 1625, but was not a popular king. He was known to have favourites among his friends, who he promoted to powerful positions, and he regarded himself as a supreme or divine ruler (i.e. accountable only to God), whose views and decisions could not be challenged by anyone. James I was also very extravagant, and he imposed heavy taxation and duties on the country without the approval of parliament.

Law

(see also **Parliament** and **Society**)

The law is the body of rules within a state or community which individuals are obliged to keep. In most societies, penalties such as fines or imprisonment, are imposed on people who break the law. In Britain, all of the rules (laws) that citizens must abide by have to be approved by parliament. Some laws of our land are very ancient, dating back to earlier centuries. Serious crimes today are tried in a Court of Law, heard by a jury and presided over by a judge.

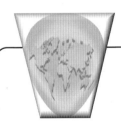

Legacy

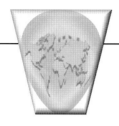

The legacy of our past is that which has been handed down or 'left' to us by people of past societies. Historic legacy includes languages, place names, **artefacts**, **myths and legends**, music, literature, and styles of art and architecture.

Lenin

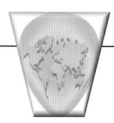

(see also **Russian Revolution**)

Vladimir Ilyich Lenin is the adopted name of Vladimir Ilyich Ulyanov, who lived from 1870 to 1924. He was the first leader of the USSR, that is, the former Union of Soviet Socialist Republics, and a leading authority on the theory of **communism**. Lenin was the leader of the Bolshevik **revolution** in 1917 and became leader of a Soviet government.

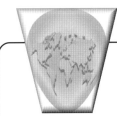

Longship

(see also **Vikings**)

A longship is the name given to the vessels of the **Vikings**, who depended on sea transport for their voyages. One of the most famous of Viking longships is the Gokstad ship, excavated in Norway in 1880. It was made of oak, with a pine mast and a large steering paddle on the right, or starboard, side of the stern. The ship had been buried in a mound of clay that had helped to preserve it. It contained the body of a dead Viking king.

Lord of the manor

(see also **Middle Ages**)

In the period of the Middle Ages, around AD1000 to 1450, most people in Europe lived in villages. The head of each village was called the Lord of the Manor. He owned the village land and lived in its grandest house called the manor house. The lord allowed the villagers to farm strips of land that they paid for by working for him and providing food for the lord and his family.

Magellan, Ferdinand

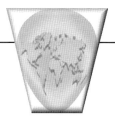

Ferdinand Magellan was a famous Portuguese navigator and explorer, who lived from 1480 to 1521. His famous voyage of 1519 to 1522 in his ship the *Victoria* met with both successes and failures. The *Victoria* sailed from Seville. It passed through what is now called the Magellan Strait at the tip of South America, crossed the ocean he named the Pacific, and reached the Philippines. There, Magellan himself was killed. The ship and crew returned home. This was the first ever expedition which sailed all around the globe. It proved beyond doubt that the world is round.

Magna Carta

The words Magna Carta are Latin. They mean the 'Greater Charter'. The Magna Carta was a document (a charter) signed by King John of England in 1215. King John had been very unpopular because he imposed very heavy taxation and made other unreasonable demands of the people. As a result, the barons, that is, the land owning noblemen of the land, made him sign the Magna Carta, which established the right of the barons to be consulted over such matters as taxation. The charter was signed at Runnymede on 15 June 1215.

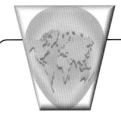

Mary, Queen of Scots

(see also **Stuarts**, **King James I** and **Queen Elizabeth I**)

Mary, Queen of Scots, also known as Mary Stuart, lived from 1542 to 1587. She was queen of Scotland from 1542 to 1567, and is probably the most famous **monarch** of Scotland. She married three times. Because of a connection with the English royal line of inheritance, she was a threat to Queen Elizabeth I. In 1567 she was forced to **abdicate** and give the throne to her young son, James (who later became King James I of England). Mary herself fled to England and became involved in plots against Queen Elizabeth I. For her role in such plots, Elizabeth held her prisoner and she was eventually executed in 1587.

Mary Rose

(see also **Henry VIII** and **Tudors**)

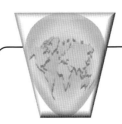

The Mary Rose was one of Henry VIII's ships, which sank when defending England against the French fleet. The wreck of the Mary Rose, recovered over 400 years later, represents one of the major sources of **evidence** of the Tudor age. **Artefacts** found on board when the ship was salvaged give us important evidence of life on board a warship of the Tudor era.

Maya

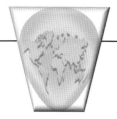

The Maya Indians were some of the earliest and greatest people of Central America. The Maya Indian civilisation originated in the Yucatán Peninsula about 2600BC. In later years they occupied sites in Mexico, Guatemala and Belize. From early beginnings in caves and simple forest homes, the Maya developed an **empire** based on cities hidden deep in the forests. They built stone buildings and pyramids and were skilful farmers, stone carvers, potters and weavers. The Maya were very religious and worshipped the earth, rain and plant and animal gods. Their empire declined around AD950.

Medieval

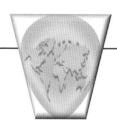

(see also **Middle Ages**)

Medieval (or Mediaeval) means relating to the Middle Ages, or the period between 'ancient' and 'modern' times. The medieval period is not specific, but is loosely used to describe times from around AD800, the time of the founding of the **Holy Roman Empire**, to the middle of the 15th century, the time of the **Renaissance**.

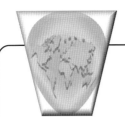

Middle Ages

(see also **Medieval**)

The Middle Ages is the period of history in Europe between the end of the **Roman Empire** and the **Renaissance**. The period is not specific, but the term generally applies to the years from the 6th century AD to the 15th century. Historians divide the Middle Ages into three shorter periods: the Early Middle Ages (5th or 6th to 11th centuries); the High Middle Ages (12th to 13th centuries); and the Later Middle Ages (14th to 15th centuries).

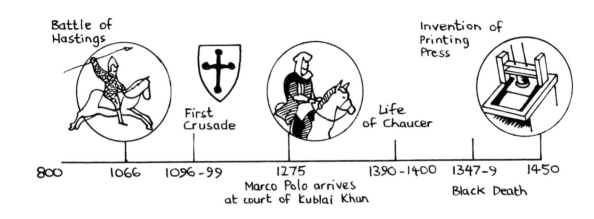

Mogul Empire

The Mogul (or Mughal) Empire was an **empire** representing an important stage in the history of the Indian sub-continent. The Mogul Empire was founded in India in the 14th century by the Mogul **dynasty** or family. The empire began in the north of the country and spread to eventually cover most of India. It began to decline in the early 18th century. The last Mogul emperor was deposed (removed from office) by the English in 1857.

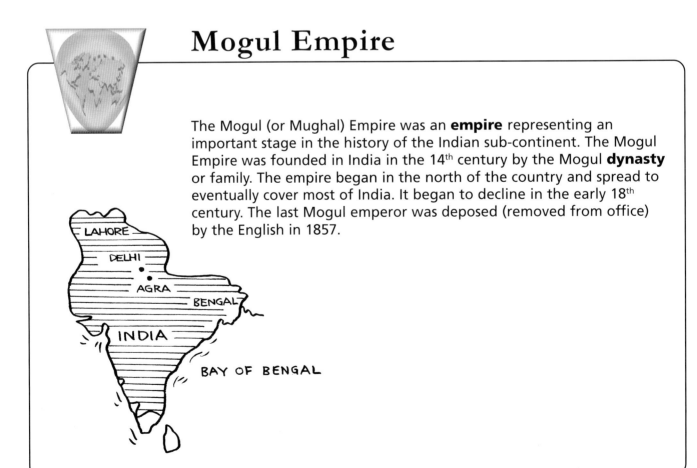

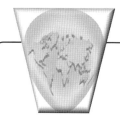

Monarch

(see also **Sovereign**)

A monarch is a sole, or absolute ruler of a state. A monarch is a sovereign, who may have the title of king, queen, emperor or empress.

The word monarchy is used to describe a state ruled by a monarch, also the rule or government exercised by the monarch.

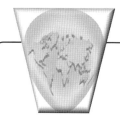

Monastery

(see also **Dissolution of the monasteries** and **King Henry VIII**)

A monastery is a place where a community of people (usually men who are termed monks) live in seclusion from the world. Monks live their lives according to strict religious vows or rules. Several centuries ago, monks were often the most educated members of a society. They learned to read Latin, the language of religious books, and often had a good knowledge of science and medicine. During the reign of King Henry VIII, many monasteries were destroyed.

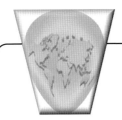

Mussolini

(see also **Fascism**)

Benito Mussolini lived from 1883 to 1945. He was Italian dictator from 1925 to 1943 and founder of the fascist movement. Mussolini was known as Il Duce or 'the leader'. In June 1940, Mussolini sided with **Hitler** and entered the **Second World War**. He was forced to resign from power in 1943 because of military and domestic failures.

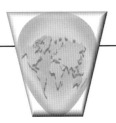

Myths and legends

(see also **Legacy**)

A myth is a fictitious account or story that often involves supernatural (extraordinary or inexplicable) events or people, yet which may incorporate an idea which concerns natural or historic matters. A legend is a historic story, passed on by tradition from one generation to the next. Legends are generally fictitious, yet are popularly regarded as historical.

Myths and legends form an important aspect of the legacy of our past. They provide insights into past ideas, events and societies.

PEGASUS

Napoleon I

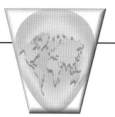

(see also **French Revolution**)

Napoleon I, or Napoleon Bonaparte, lived from 1769 to 1821. He was Emperor of the French from 1804 to 1814 and 1814 to 1815. Napoleon was a general in the wars of the French Revolution, and in 1799 he overthrew the rulers and made himself dictator. From 1803, Napoleon conquered most of Europe in what are known as the Napoleonic Wars. Eventually, in 1815, he was defeated by the British army in the Battle of Waterloo. He then went to live in exile on the island of St Helena.

Nationalism

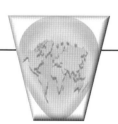

(see also **Imperialism**)

Nationalism is a political policy of national independence. It is a movement that aims to unify a nation, or free it from imperialist rule. Nationalist movements were powerful in Europe in the 19th century, for example, in Germany and Italy. Nationalists believe in their country's right to remain independent from other countries.

Nazis

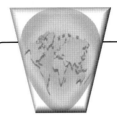

(see also **Hitler**, **Second World War** and **Holocaust**)

Nazis are members of a political party known as the nazi party. Its full name in German is Nationalsozialistich Deutsche Arbeiterpartei, or the National Socialist German Workers' Party. Nazis support racism, **nationalism**, and the supremacy of the state over the individual. Many similar parties were created throughout Europe and the USA in the 1930s. The German nazi party was responsible for the German occupation of Europe during the Second World War, and the holocaust. After this war the party was banned in Germany. Today, parties with similar ideas and beliefs exist throughout the world.

Newton, Isaac

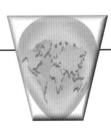

Sir Isaac Newton was one of the greatest scientists in the world. Newton, an Englishman, lived from 1642 to 1727. His discoveries changed people's ideas about the universe. He discovered and established laws of light and motion and formulated the law of gravity.

Nobility

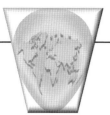

Nobility is a word used to describe those people or ranks in a **society** who have certain hereditary privileges, such as the inheritance of great wealth, property or 'title' such as Lord. The wealth of the nobility has traditionally been derived from the land. In many societies, until very recently (ie 20th century), leading figures of governments and armies came from the nobility.

Norman Conquest

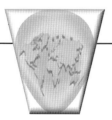

(see also **Battle of Hastings**, **Bayeux Tapestry** and **Normans**)

The Norman Conquest is the term used to describe the **conquest** of England by the Normans. In 1066 King Edward the Confessor of England died. He was succeeded by Harold, Earl of Wessex. Yet two other people wished to claim the throne of England: William, Duke of Normandy, and Harold Hardrada of Norway. Harold Hardrada invaded England but was defeated. Shortly afterwards, William of Normandy invaded and was successful. He defeated the Saxons in the Battle of Hastings.

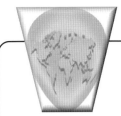

Normans

(see also **Norman Conquest**)

The Normans, or 'northmen' were descendants of the **Vikings**. They settled in northern France during the 9th century. In AD911 they accepted the French king as their overlord (supreme lord and master) and converted to Christianity. In return, they gained control of the region of northern France we know as Normandy.

NORMAN KNIGHT

NORMAN CASTLE

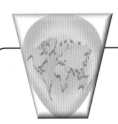

Odin

(see also **Vikings**)

Odin was the most important of the many Viking gods. Alternative names for him are Woden and the All-Father. From his name is derived the Wednesday (Woden's Day) of our week. From his throne in the Norse heaven known as Asgard, Odin could see out all over the world. According to legend, Odin had an eight legged horse. He was regarded as the wisest of the gods. Legend tells us that he sacrificed one eye in his constant quest for knowledge. At dawn each day his two ravens, Hugin and Munin (Mind and Memory), were let out to fly around the world and report back to Odin on what they had found.

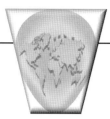

Ottoman Empire

The Ottoman Empire is the name given to the Muslim empire of the Turks. It lasted between 1300 and 1920. It was founded by the Turkish rule Osman I or Othman I. The empire reached its greatest extent under the rule of the Ottoman Sultan Suleiman in the 16th century. Suleiman invaded and made conquests in the Balkans, the Mediterranean area, Persia and North Africa. During the 17th century the empire began its decline. The capital of the Ottoman Empire as from 1453 was Istanbul, formerly called Constantinople.

Pagan

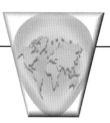

Pagan is a word used in the first instance by **Christians** to describe a person who was not a follower of Christ and who worshipped gods other than the Christian God.

PAGAN ANIMAL SYMBOLS

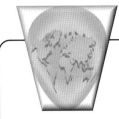

Parliament

(see also **Law** and **Government**)

The word parliament comes from the French word 'parler', meaning to speak. In England, a parliament or meeting for speaking about matters of government was first called in 1264. Various knights and spokesmen from the towns were invited to attend. In 1332, parliament first met in two buildings or 'houses', the House of Lords attended by clergy and nobility, and the House of Commons, attended by representatives from towns and shires. By 1600 all laws of the land had to be approved by both Houses as they still do in modern times.

The two Houses of Parliament are today the 'Great Council' or supreme government of the United Kingdom. The word 'parliament' is now used in other countries also to describe the government of the nation.

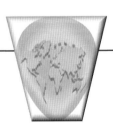

Persian Wars

The term Persian Wars refers to a series of conflicts between Greece and Persia. The wars took place between 499 and 449BC. Greece eventually won the wars. This was an important turning point in world history. It marked the end of the time when Persia dominated the ancient world.

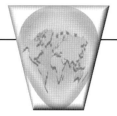

Peter the Great

(see also **Tsar**)

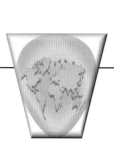

Peter the Great was the first of three men named Peter who were tsars of Russia. Peter I was born in 1672 and became tsar from 1682, when his brother Tsar Feodor died. From 1689 he controlled the government of Russia. He worked hard to change many aspects of life in the country so they were more modern or 'westernised'. For example, he modernised the army, built new ships, changed administrative systems and encouraged education. He built a new capital city, named St Petersburg. Peter the Great died in 1725.

Pharaohs

(see also **Ancient Egypt** and **Tutankhamun**)

The word pharaoh means 'great house', perhaps palace. The pharaohs were the god-kings of Ancient Egypt – the people viewed their kings as gods and believed that their personal powers caused the annual flooding of the River Nile (crucial for farming). Out of respect, the Egyptians would not refer to their god-king by name, and so they used the word pharaoh – for example, to explain that 'the palace has ordered' something to be done. The king had absolute power over the land and the people. He commanded the Egyptian army, and was also the chief priest. Queen Hatshepsut was one of the few women pharaohs of Egypt.

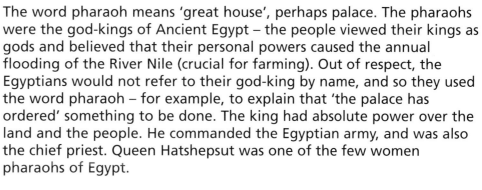

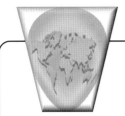

Prehistoric

Prehistoric means belonging to the period of time before historic events were written or otherwise recorded. Historians have to rely on **evidence** such as the finds of archaeologists in order to understand prehistoric societies. Discoveries, such as cave paintings in southern France and Spain, help to give us some idea about the lives of people in 'prehistory'.

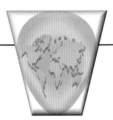

Prophet Muhammad

Muhammad (or Mohammed or Mahomet) lived from 570 to 632. He was born in Mecca on the Arabian peninsula and was the founder of Islam, one of the major religious faiths of the world. Around 616 Muhammad claimed to be a prophet. He said that the Koran was revealed to him by God. The Koran was later written down by Muhammad's followers.

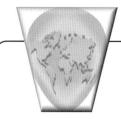

Queen Elizabeth I

(see also **Tudors** and **Mary, Queen of Scots**)

Queen Elizabeth I lived from 1533 to 1603. She became queen of England in 1558 when **Queen Mary I** died. Elizabeth was the daughter of **King Henry VIII** and Anne Boleyn. She made England (previously Roman Catholic) into a Protestant country once again and enforced Protestantism by law. Elizabeth's reign is noted for its expansion and success in exploration and discovery of the world, in commerce, and in literature and the arts. During her reign, England defeated the Spanish in the **Armada**.

Elizabeth had no children. She executed one of her rivals, Mary, Queen of Scots, and named Mary's Protestant son James as her heir (who became **King James I** of England).

{**Armada**: *n.* a fleet of armed ships, esp. that sent by Philip II of Spain against England in 1588. *Chambers.* See the entry for Armada ... that makes sense!]

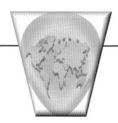

Queen Elizabeth II

(see also **Windsor**)

Elizabeth II, born in 1926, has been queen of Great Britain and Northern Ireland since 1952. She is the elder daughter of King George VI. Elizabeth became queen on the death of her father and was crowned on 2 June 1953. She is married to Philip, the Duke of Edinburgh. They have four children: Charles, who is heir to the throne, Anne, Andrew and Edward.

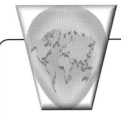

Queen Mary I

(see also **Tudors**)

Mary Tudor, or Queen Mary I, lived from 1516 to 1558 and was queen of England from 1553 until her death. She married a Catholic prince, named Philip, who was heir to the throne in Spain. Mary was determined to make England a Catholic country once again following the break with Rome in the **Reformation**. Her attempts at restoring Catholicism involved the arrest and persecution of Protestants. During her reign, 300 Protestants were burned at the stake for refusing to become Roman Catholics. Queen Mary I is nicknamed 'Bloody Mary'.

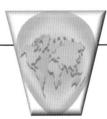

Queen Victoria

Victoria, granddaughter of King George III and niece of King William IV, became queen of England on the death of her Uncle William in 1837. She was eighteen years old when she became queen. In 1840, Victoria married Prince Albert of Saxe-Coburg and Gotha. They had four sons and five daughters. Queen Victoria died in 1901. Her long life and reign saw very many changes and advancements – in such things as general ways of life, agriculture, industry and technology. The so-called 'Victorian era' or ' Victorian age' is one of great historical significance. Queen Victoria had the longest reign of any British **monarch**.

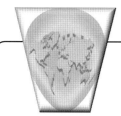

Reformation

(see also **King Henry VIII** and **Act of Supremacy**)

The term Reformation describes a political and religious movement that took place in Europe in the 16th century. The movement's aim was to make radical changes to (reform) the Roman Catholic church. The Reformation led to the establishment of Protestant churches. In England, King Henry VIII played a key role in the Reformation. He renounced the supremacy of the Pope and in the Act of Supremacy, declared himself head of the Church of England.

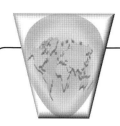

Regent

A Regent is someone, usually a relative, who rules on behalf of the **monarch** if he or she is unable to rule. A Regent may be appointed if the monarch is too young to rule, or perhaps too ill to rule. In British history, for example, the son of George III acted as Prince Regent during the last years of his father's, King George III, life, because the king was too ill to rule.

GEORGE IV, PRINCE REGENT

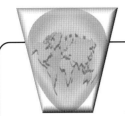

Renaissance

During the 15th century, people in Italy began to develop new ideas about the world and to take great interest in art, literature, music, learning, and the cultural **legacy** of the 'great' past civilisations of **Ancient Greece** and Rome. They revived Greek and Roman ideas in this time of 'Renaissance', meaning revival or rebirth. From its beginnings in Italy, the Renaissance spread across Europe. Many new schools and universities were founded during this period and it was a time of very significant achievement in culture and the arts. Famous figures of the Renaissance include Leonardo **da Vinci**, Michelangelo and William Shakespeare.

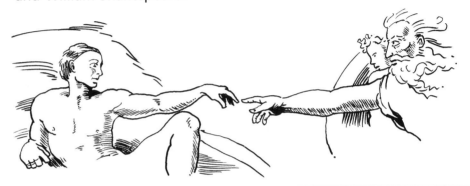

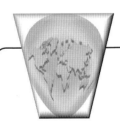

Republic

A republic is a state or country without a king, queen or emperor. A Republic is governed by elected representatives or an elected president. Republics have existed throughout history. An example from ancient times is the **Roman** republic. Modern day republics include the Republic of Singapore, the People's Republic of China, France and the United States of America.

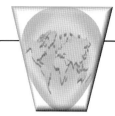

Restoration

(see also **Stuarts**, **English civil war** and Oliver **Cromwell**)

The term Restoration describes the period in the history of England when the Stuart monarchy was restored after the English civil war had ended and the Protectorate of Oliver Cromwell had fallen. Cromwell died in 1658, his son Richard succeeded him but was a very ineffective ruler. In 1660 parliament restored the monarchy and Charles II (son of **Charles I**), became king of England. At the time of the Restoration, parliament limited the powers of the monarchy and increased its own powers.

CHARLES II

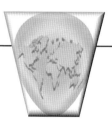

Revolution

(see also **American War of Independence**, **Russian Revolution** and **French Revolution**)

A revolution is the word used by historians to describe any rapid, violent or great change in a society. Usually the term refers to sudden and far reaching political changes. It could also refer to rapid social or economic changes.

Roman Conquest

(see also **Romans** and **Julius Caesar**)

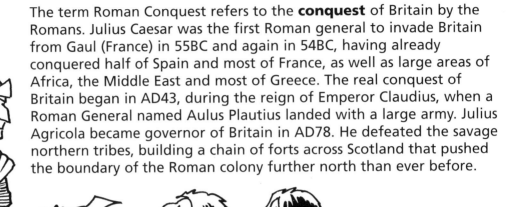

The term Roman Conquest refers to the **conquest** of Britain by the Romans. Julius Caesar was the first Roman general to invade Britain from Gaul (France) in 55BC and again in 54BC, having already conquered half of Spain and most of France, as well as large areas of Africa, the Middle East and most of Greece. The real conquest of Britain began in AD43, during the reign of Emperor Claudius, when a Roman General named Aulus Plautius landed with a large army. Julius Agricola became governor of Britain in AD78. He defeated the savage northern tribes, building a chain of forts across Scotland that pushed the boundary of the Roman colony further north than ever before.

Romans

(see also **Roman Conquest** and **Julius Caesar**)

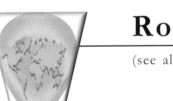

The first Romans were the native people of Rome in Italy. People first entered Italy around 2000BC. Rome was founded in 753BC. From a small village set on one of seven hills, Rome developed into a major city, and a republic. The history of ancient Rome is one of almost continuous expansion from the founding of Rome until the death of Julius Caesar and the foundation of the Roman Empire under Emperor Augustus in 27BC. At its greatest, the **empire** stretched from Britain to Mesopotamia and the Caspian Sea. The civilisation of ancient Rome had great influence on the whole of Western Europe and beyond. Its **legacy** is in such fields as art, architecture, literature, language, law and engineering.

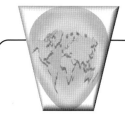

Russian Revolution

(see also **Revolution** and **Lenin**)

The Russian Revolution of 1917 was a time of major civil unrest and political change in Russia. In the spring of that year, the Romanov **dynasty** was overthrown. Tsar Nicholas II abdicated. Later in the year, the Bolshevik political party, headed up by Lenin, established a **communist** soviet state, to be called the Union of Soviet Socialist Republics (USSR). In 1918, the Bolsheviks changed their name to the Russian Communist Party. The constitution of the USSR was adopted in 1923.

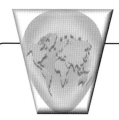

Second World War

(see also **Hitler**, **Nazis**, **Battle of Britain**, **Allied Powers**, **Blitz**, **Holocaust** and **Hiroshima**)

The Second World War lasted from 1939 until 1945. It was a **war** between the Axis Powers of Germany, Italy and Japan, and the Allied Powers. It began in September 1939 when Germany invaded Poland. Britain and France then declared war on Germany and the USSR invaded Poland. Many battles were waged during the war, including the Battle of Britain. It is estimated that fifty five million people died during the course of the war. In May 1945, Germany surrendered to the Allied Powers, but Japan continued fighting until after the USA dropped atomic bombs on Hiroshima and Nagasaki in August 1945.

Settlement

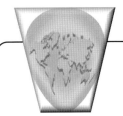

A settlement is a place where a number of people live or have lived. It may describe a pre-historic dwelling place, a small village or collection of houses, or a town or city. The word settlement is also used to refer to a place where immigrants or colonists have made their home in a new country away from their homeland.

Shih Huang Ti

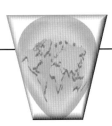

Shih Huang Ti, or Shi Huangdi, lived from 259 to 210BC, and was the first emperor of China. Until the unification of China by Shih Huang Ti, it had been divided into several rival states. Shih Huang Ti was the first of a family line or **dynasty** of emperors called the Ch'in Emperors. When he became emperor in 221BC, he built the Great Wall of China. The wall still stands today and is around 2,710km in length.

Slavery

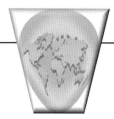

Slavery means the enforced servitude of one person, a slave, to another person – or of a group of slaves to another group of 'masters'. Slaves are forced to do what their master tells them. They have no personal rights. They are the property of their master through birth, capture or purchase. Slavery has existed since ancient times. It was abolished in the **British Empire** in 1833, and in the United States of America at the end of the **American Civil War**. Today slavery goes on illegally in some countries of the world.

Society

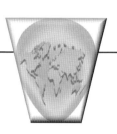

The word society is used to describe a group or collection of people who have come to live together in a community for mutual benefits. Generally, people in a society live according to agreed customs or rules. In early or traditional societies, people tended to accept the rules and not to challenge them. A feature of a modern society is that there are mechanisms for discussing and changing rules and laws that individuals are expected to abide by.

Sovereign

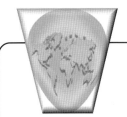

(see also **Monarch**)

A sovereign is a monarch or other recognised ruler who holds 'sovereignty', that is, supreme authority over a country.

A sovereign state is a state that rules itself; that is, it is independent of outside authority.

Space age

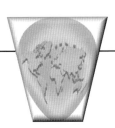

The space age refers to the era of modern history in which people have been capable of launching flying craft into space, beyond the atmosphere of the Earth. The earliest craft, *Sputnik I*, was launched by the USSR in 1957. In 1961 Yuri Gagarin of the USSR became the first man to make a space flight, and Valentina Tereschkova of the USSR became the first woman to fly in space in 1963. In 1969 Neil Armstrong and Edwin 'Buzz' Aldrin of the USA became the first men to walk on the surface of the moon – having been taken there by their craft, *Apollo II*.

Spanish conquest

The term Spanish conquest refers to the **conquest** of the **Aztec civilisation** by Spain, brought about by the voyage of Hernando Cortes to Mexico in 1519. Cortes landed in Mexico with a force of about 500 soldiers, fifteen horses, thirteen muskets, and seven small cannon. Once the force had disembarked, Cortes took the decision to burn all the ships so there could be no turning back from the course he had set for the expedition – the conquest of the Aztecs. Cortes governed the country for the next seven years. Soon the Spaniards conquered the whole of Mexico and named it New Spain.

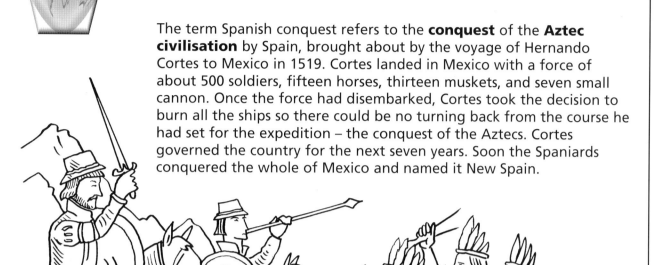

Stalin

(see also **Communism** and **Russian Revolution**)

Joseph Stalin was a Soviet politician who lived from 1879 until 1953. He became secretary of the communist party in 1922. After **Lenin** died in 1924, Stalin clashed with rival Soviet Trotsky and was successful in his bid to become ruler of the Union of Society Socialist Republics (USSR). Stalin remained as **dictator** until his death in 1953.

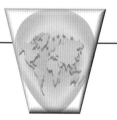

Steam power

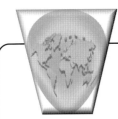

(see also **Industrial Revolution**)

During the 18th century in Britain, steam was discovered and developed as a source of power. This crucial discovery led to the rapid development of industry. Steam power revolutionised **transport** and the production of coal and cotton cloth in Britain. It also led to the establishment of new industries. In 1782, James Watt designed a rotary steam engine, and in 1804 the first steam engine was built to run along a rail track.

Stone Age

The earliest people, known as Old Stone Age people, lived in caves. They hunted animals and gathered plants for food. Their tools and weapons were made out of flint and bone. The first **evidence** of Old Stone Age, or Palaeolithic era, people in Britain dates from about 15000BC. Later, around 4000BC, people arrived in Britain from mainland Europe and developed farming techniques. People built huts out of stone or wood, and cleared land to graze animals and grow plants for food. This later Stone Age period is known as the New Stone Age, or Neolithic era.

Stuarts

(see also **Mary, Queen of Scots, King James I, King Charles I** and **Restoration**)

The Stuarts (or Stewarts) are the family or **house of history** that inherited the throne of Scotland in 1371 and the throne of England in 1603. The most famous Scottish Stewart **monarch** was Mary, Queen of Scots. Her son, James, became King James VI of Scotland in 1567 when he was only a year old. In 1603 Queen Elizabeth I made James VI her heir. When Elizabeth died in 1603, James became king of both Scotland and England (King James I). From that time onwards, the same monarch has ruled over both countries. The Stuart monarchs that ruled after King James I are Charles I, Charles II, James II, William III and Mary II (who jointly ruled), and Queen Anne. The Stuart **dynasty** ended with the death of Queen Anne in 1714.

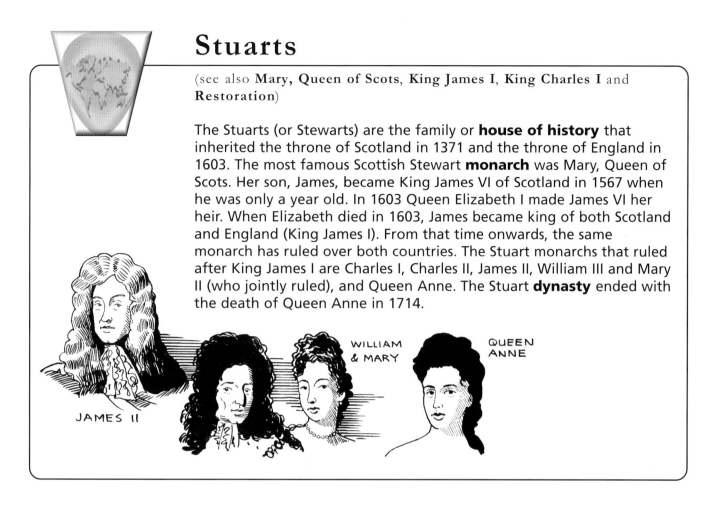

JAMES II

WILLIAM & MARY

QUEEN ANNE

Suez Canal

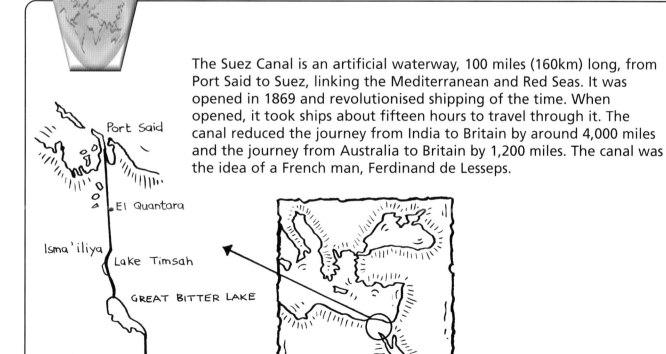

The Suez Canal is an artificial waterway, 100 miles (160km) long, from Port Said to Suez, linking the Mediterranean and Red Seas. It was opened in 1869 and revolutionised shipping of the time. When opened, it took ships about fifteen hours to travel through it. The canal reduced the journey from India to Britain by around 4,000 miles and the journey from Australia to Britain by 1,200 miles. The canal was the idea of a French man, Ferdinand de Lesseps.

Port Said

El Quantara

Isma'iliya

Lake Timsah

GREAT BITTER LAKE

Suez

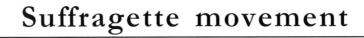

Suffragette movement

Suffragettes is the term used to describe women who campaigned for the right to vote in parliamentary elections. Women had very few legal rights until the early 20th century. In 1903, Emmeline and Christabel Pankhurst established the Women's Social and Political Union which set about campaigning for the rights of women. Some members of the movement were punished by imprisonment for their demonstrations and other activities. Eventually, the movement achieved success. In 1919 women over the age of thirty were given the right to vote. In 1928 the age limit was lowered to twenty one, making it the same as for men.

Sumerians

(see also **Assyrian Empire**)

The Sumerians are people who belonged to the world's earliest civilisation, the Sumerian civilisation, which began around 3200BC. This civilisation began in the area between the Tigris and Euphrates rivers in the part of the world known as Mesopotamia, meaning "the land between two rivers". Today, this area is in the country of Iraq. From early beginnings, a great civilisation developed, based on the city states. The great cities included Lagash, Eridu, Uruk and Ur. The Sumerians constructed huge temple-towers, built up on platforms. They are the people who developed the earliest form of writing.

ZIGGURAT OF UR-NAMMU

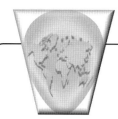

Trade

(see also **Industrial Revolution**)

Trade is the exchange of goods and other services for economic benefit. Items may be traded between individuals or businesses within a country or between countries. Railways, roads, rivers and canals serve as important over-land trade routes. Cargo ships carry goods that are imported and exported across the oceans, and aeroplanes convey light goods, mail and passengers across the trade routes of the air.

The Industrial Revolution was a time of rapid development in **transport** and opportunities for trade.

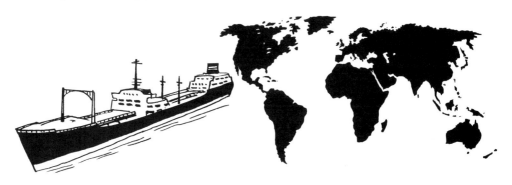

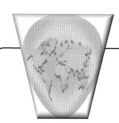

Transport

(see also **Industrial Revolution**)

To transport means to convey people or goods by land or sea or air. Forms of transport include bicycle, car, truck, train, hovercraft, ferry, tanker, barge, ocean liner and jet aircraft. Transport moves along transportation routes, which include roads, railway lines, canals, and agreed shipping and air routes. The period of the Industrial Revolution resulted in significant developments in forms and speed of transport.

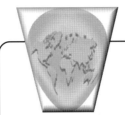

Treason

Treason is the crime of betraying the **monarch** or government of a country. Well known people in British history who have been executed for the crime of treason include **Mary, Queen of Scots, Guy Fawkes** and **King Charles I**.

Tsar

(see also **Russian Revolution**)

The Tsar is the term that was used to describe the supreme ruler or emperor of Russia until the Russian Revolution of 1917.

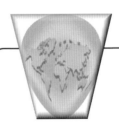

TSAR NICHOLAS II

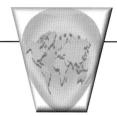

Tudors

The Tudors were one of the important houses of history in Britain. Members of the Tudor family reigned over England from 1485 to 1603. The first Tudor **monarch** was **King Henry VII**. Other reigning Tudors were **King Henry VIII**, King Edward VI, Lady Jane Grey, **Queen Mary I** and **Queen Elizabeth I**.

HENRY VII
HENRY VIII
MARY I

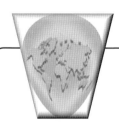

Tutankhamun

(see also **Ancient Egypt** and **Pharaohs**)

Tutankhamun was a boy-king of Ancient Egypt whose tomb survived the activities of thieves. His tomb was discovered in 1922 by an archaeologist and provides tremendously important **evidence** of the days of the pharaohs. In a solid gold coffin lay the body of the young king. Other treasures found in the tomb include bangles and bracelets, rings, models of ships, perfume caskets, gilt statuettes of gods, decorated chests, other furniture, chariots with golden wheels, and a royal throne. The tomb was guarded by a life sized statue of Tutankhamun himself.

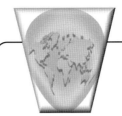

United Nations

The United Nations is an association of states set up in 1945 with the aim of promoting international peace and co-operation. The association was established at the end of the **Second World War**. Many people at the time, and indeed today, believed that there are better ways to promote peace and resolve international disagreements than by military **conflict**, involving the violent death of many human beings.

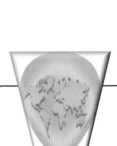

Venerable Bede

(see also **AD**)

Bede, otherwise known as the Venerable Bede, lived from around 673 to 735. He was an extremely influential English historian and theologian. Bede was influential for many reasons, particularly because of his ability as a writer. His famous work on the **history** of the church and Saxon England, called *Ecclesiastical History of the English People*, is a major source of **evidence** about the period which historians have consulted throughout the centuries. The Venerable Bede was particularly active in Durham and Northumbria.

Victory

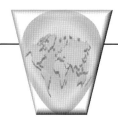

(see also **War**)

Victory is the position of having beaten or overcome an enemy in a battle or war. It is a state of superiority achieved as a result of armed **conflict**.

Vikings

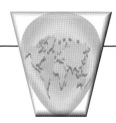

(see also **Longship** and **Odin**)

Vikings, otherwise known as Norsemen, were **medieval** Scandinavian sea warriors, who invaded and settled in Britain and other countries in Europe. The Viking age in Britain began in AD789, when ships first appeared off the coast, and ended after 1066 when the **Normans** won the **Battle of Hastings**. The word Viking probably derives from the Scandinavian words 'vik' or 'vig', meaning an inlet from the sea, a creek or fjord, and 'ing' meaning people

War

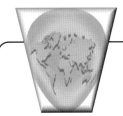

A war is a prolonged fight or hostile contest between armed forces. A war may be carried on between nations, states or rulers, or between opposing parties in the same nation or state.

Wars of the Roses

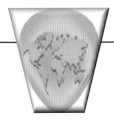

The Wars of the Roses is the name given to the various battles or struggles for power between two royal houses of history – the houses of York and Lancaster. The wars are named after the emblems of the two rivals: the white rose of York and the red rose of Lancaster. Both rival houses claimed the throne through descent from the sons of King Edward III. Fighting broke out in 1455 and ended at the Battle of Bosworth in 1485, when the Yorkist regime ended. In this battle, Henry Tudor defeated King Richard III and became **Henry VII** of England.

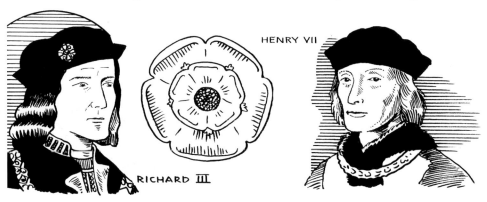

HENRY VII

RICHARD III

Welfare state

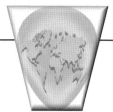

Welfare state is a political system within which the state has responsibility for the welfare of its citizens rather than the individual or private bodies. In a welfare state, services such as sickness benefits, family allowances, medical care, education and unemployment benefits are provided through state insurance schemes and taxes. The welfare state in Britain began during the period of government by the Labour Party that began in 1945, led by prime minister Clement Attlee. The establishment of the welfare state was followed, in 1948, by the setting up of the National Health Service, which provides free medical care for all citizens.

CLEMENT ATTLEE

Windsor

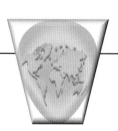

(see also **Queen Elizabeth II**)

The House of Windsor is the official name of the royal family of Britain since 1917. It is therefore the most recent and current **house of history** in Britain. The name Windsor was adopted instead of Saxe-Coburg, the previous family name deriving from **Queen Victoria's** husband Prince Albert of Saxe-Coburg. Monarchs of the House of Windsor are King George V, King Edward VIII, King George VI and Queen Elizabeth II.

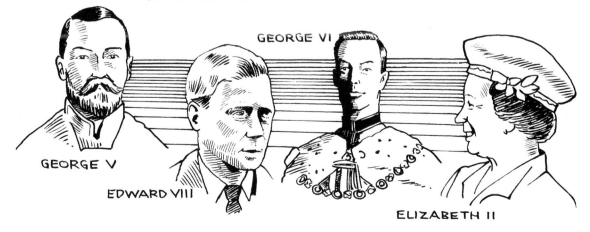

GEORGE VI

GEORGE V

EDWARD VIII

ELIZABETH II

Also available from Questions...

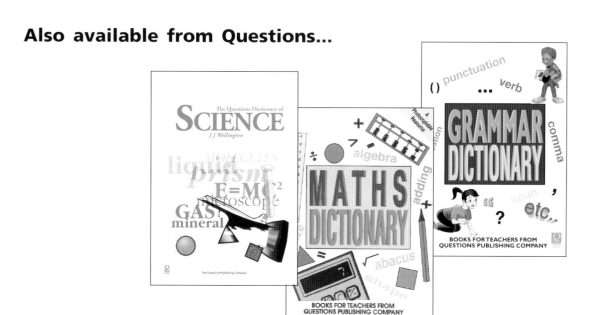

QUESTIONS' BEST-SELLING SUBJECT DICTIONARIES

SCIENCE DICTIONARY

By Jerry Wellington

An innovative dictionary that helps to shed lights on what can often be a confusing vocabulary for children to understand. The key scientific terms are explained in full rather than just defined, with examples and diagrams throughout.

ISBN: 1-898149-84-4 Price: £12.99

MATHS DICTIONARY

By Kev Delaney, Adrian Pinel and Derek Smith

An A-Z of key mathematical ideas and concepts, including clear illustrations and examples that explain the words specific to mathematics.

ISBN: 1-898149-70-4 Price: £12.99

GRAMMAR DICTIONARY

By Mary Mason

Providing definitions of key grammatical terms and concepts in a way that demonstrates their usefulness and validity. Fully illustrated throughout.

ISBN: 1-898149-81-X Price: £12.99

If you would like to place an order for these publications or would like to receive more information on the full range of products available from Questions Publishing Limited you can phone us on **0121 212 0919** or fax us on **0121 212 0959** or write to us at: The Questions Publishing Company Limited, Customer Services, 27 Frederick Street, Birmingham B1 3HH.

Also available from Questions...

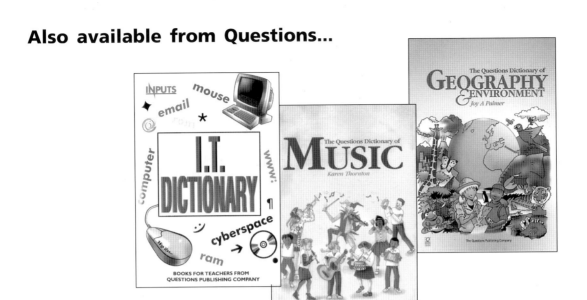

QUESTIONS' BEST-SELLING SUBJECT DICTIONARIES

IT DICTIONARY

By Colin Rouse

Information Communications Technology (ICT) opens up new horizons for children, but is surrounded by jargon that can sometimes act as a barrier to learning. Far more than just a collection of words and definitions, the *IT Dictionary* is an essential introduction for children to the world of ICT.

ISBN: 1-899149-78-X Price: £12.99

MUSIC DICTIONARY

By Karren Thornton

Over 150 key musical terms are defined using accessible language for the non-expert. Useful for musical beginners of any age, each entry is fully illustrated, providing a valuable insight into words and meanings that are not always found in traditional dictionaries.

ISBN: 1-898149-85-2 Price: £15.99

GEOGRAPHY & ENVIRONMENT DICTIONARY

By Joy Palmer

An essential reference source for Key Stage 3 classrooms, the *Geography & Environment Dictionary* introduces children to key geographical vocabulary and specialist terms. The dictionary is fully illustrated with clearly worded explanations for each entry.

ISBN: 1-84190-031-1 Price: £12.99

If you would like to place an order for these publications or would like to receive more information on the full range of products available from Questions Publishing Limited you can phone us on **0121 212 0919** or fax us on **0121 212 0959** or write to us at: The Questions Publishing Company Limited, Customer Services, 27 Frederick Street, Birmingham B1 3HH.